PURSUING PURPOSE

PURSUING PURPOSE

Living Life With Purpose, On Purpose, and For Purpose

LOIS HARMON

IMPACT

COPYRIGHT

Front Cover design by Dynasty Solutions, Back Cover Design by Pump Up the Violet Publishing, author photograph by IMPACT, hairstylist: Christine Fowler.

Published by IMPACT, Rocklin, CA, 95765

First edition: April 2023

Library of Congress Control Number: 2023902839

ISBN-13: 9798987525401

PRAISE FOR PURSUING PURPOSE

Dr. Lois Harmon has put together a comprehensive, encouraging, challenging itinerary for the person who is pursuing purpose in life. She could have called her work "Striving for Purpose," implying that our human intellect and effort are the keys to arriving at a desired destination, that is, that enough human sweat and effort could safely get us to our destination. She could have titled her book "Finding Purpose" implying that life purpose is a nugget of gold that only the few "lucky ones" discover thus discouraging most people from even bothering to attempt the journey. Pursuing certainly carries with it the necessity of human effort. However, that human effort is motivated, finetuned, and developed by loving Father God who desires that we all fulfill our purpose in Him.

Thank you, Dr. Harmon, that, in your own journey with the Lord, you have discovered that a part of your purpose is to assist others on their journeys as well.

-Reverend Dr. Calvin Daniel Austin, Pastor of The Oaks Church, Gainesville, Fl

Dr. Lois Harmon provides a masterfully written and expository narrative in this awe-inspiring publication. Divine revelation flows out of every paragraph with empowering tenets of living on purpose, with purpose, and for purpose.

~ Dr. Dawnette Banks, CEO & Founder, Dreamcast Educational Consulting

In her book, *Pursuing Purpose*, the author guides the reader through an in-depth analysis of how our shortcomings and fears in life are overcome by action faith. She masterfully walks the reader through the Bible, highlighting scriptures and thoughts that help us to visualize and understand how our fears hamper our faith and ultimately our relationship with God. The author presents both Bible stories and modern-day examples as well as strategies to assist the reader in understanding that the challenges we face in life only serve to makes us stronger when we overcome fear and exercise on faith.

-Dr. Genniver C. Bell, Retired Professor and Higher Education Administrator

As we grow in relationship and transformation with Jesus Christ, we sync up our lives with His purpose; developed and fine-tuned by the Master Himself! Dr. Harmon's *Pursuing Purpose* takes us on this real-life journey. The adventure of a lifetime!

"Come, follow me," Jesus said. In *Pursuing Purpose*, readers will understand what it's like in today's world to follow Jesus! Both a profound piece of literature and a book that makes you stop, reflect and take-action, *Pursuing Purpose* will have you overcoming fear through a growing faith, as you envision your life. By it, Dr. Harmon instills in readers the importance and power of prayer and God's Word for this expedition.

-Lisa C. Kraft, North America Young Adult Advisor, Community Bible Study (CBS); CBS Teaching Director, Roseville, CA (2015-2021)

CONTENTS

AUTHOR'S NOTE

Every person on the planet has a God-given purpose and every person either pursues that purpose or lives aimlessly.

People who aim at nothing in life usually strike it, which results in feeling miserable and unfulfilled. However, that's *not* God's desire for you.

Like many, you may take pride in your job, taking care of your financial obligations and other priorities, having resolved: that *is* your purpose in life. Why? Because people tend to equate who they are with what they do, or define themselves by their occupations and possessions.

Unfortunately, most people live aimlessly—unaware of why they're working for their employers, just as their employers wonder why they're in business. It's an unending cycle: employers employ people to do jobs to make profits, and employees work for companies to take care of their personal responsibilities, but no one questions if purpose is being fulfilled outside of occupational responsibilities and organizational profits.

Thankfully, God created you to live a purpose-filled life—a life that is intentional and meaningful—regardless of your past or current circumstances. He has a grand plan that involves you pursuing your purpose and obtaining success by His standards, and He desires to reveal those to you. It's time to understand God's plan for your life and pursue the purpose He created you for. This enables you to confidently live according to God's plan for your life.

This book explores the amazing benefits of pursuing purpose. Drawing from the truth of God's Word and personal experiences, I share insights to help you recognize and understand God's will and purpose for your life.

Pursuing purpose is not haphazard, but is constant, intentional, and a meaningful effort to obtain what is desired. When you pursue your God-given purpose, you holistically maximize your life—spiritually, physically, emotionally, mentally, and relationally.

In this book, I hope to share with you that you can learn to identify your purpose by understanding God's plan for your life. This book covers spiritual and practical aspects of pursuing purpose that will encourage you to live a life worthy of the calling you have received (Ephesians 4:1).

INTRODUCTION

People want to know what their purpose is in life. They want to feel they have value.

Joyce Meyer

Do you ever wonder why God created you the way He did? Why you have the temperament and personality you have? What about your favorite type of weather, place to live, work, and/or vacation? Why are they ideal for you? Are you a morning person or a night owl? Are you a commuter, or do you need close proximity and convenience in order to be comfortable? Why do you have certain hobbies and specific pet peeves? Why are you wired the way you are? Perhaps the answers to these questions reveal things relevant to your purpose.

From the commencement of this book, I want to emphasize that pursuing purpose is the greatest way to please God. God entrusts everyone with a purpose, but He does not enforce it upon anyone. However, He desires that all people choose to pursue purpose so that we do not live aimlessly. 2 Timothy 1:9 (ESV) asserts, God "saved us and called us to a holy calling, not because of our works but because of His own purpose and grace, which He gave us in Christ Jesus before the ages began." Every human being has a God-given purpose, and when you pursue that purpose, you have a clear objective and direction for living a fulfilling life.

I cannot think of a more important topic to write about than pursuing God-given purpose. It is vital because in order to reach your destiny, you have to know what your purpose is and what it means to pursue it. Understanding and pursuing your purpose are accompanied by countless amazing benefits! When you pursue purpose, you experience an exciting life of fruitfulness.

Our enemy, Satan, persistently aims to nullify our purposeful pursuit. He tempts us with false promises of satisfaction and worldly suggestions or metrics of success to judge our efforts by. He offers countless distractions and temptations to veer us off course, and he tempts us with fear and doubt, all to hinder us from pursuing purpose. Sadly, many people live according to secular standards for success in their pursuit of purpose, which are misaligned with God's will.

The Apostle Paul said, "I do not account my life of any value nor as precious to myself, if only I may finish my course and the ministry that I received from the Lord Jesus...." (Acts 20:24 [ESV]). The heavenly Father longs for each person, like the Apostle Paul, to live as a believer in whatever situation He has assigned respectively, just as God has called (see 1 Corinthians 7:17). Only then can we pursue purpose as God intends. However, Scripture promises that "the gifts and the calling of God are irrevocable." (Romans [11:29]). Merriam-Webster's 1828 dictionary defines calling as "a strong inner impulse toward a particular course of action especially when accompanied by conviction of divine influence." There is nothing more tragic than being unwilling to take the course of action God has laid out for us and longs for us to align with. So, you must carefully self-examine to discover whether or not you are pursuing the purpose God intends. You should never be satisfied if you are not pursuing your God-given purpose.

Divine Influence

God is above creation and unconstrained by gravity, time, or space. He is omniscient. God is El Roi—the God who sees, for He is always near (Deuteronomy 4:7) and concerned about you. He breathes over your situations before you encounter them. He strategically places you where you need to be and positions you to do and receive His best. It is not just in one aspect, but all aspects of your life. The Bible says, "From one man He made every nation of the human race to inhabit the entire earth, determining their set times and the fixed limits of the places where they would live." (Acts 17:26, NET).

Understanding the full scope of your purpose has little to do with how much you currently know, but everything to do with God's omniscience and plan. God affirmed this truth when He openly confessed, ".... I am God, and there is none like me. Only I can tell you the future before it even happens. Everything I plan will come to pass, for I do whatever I wish." (Isaiah 46:9–10, NLT). None of us are capable of manifesting God's will on our own, but we can partner with Him as we pursue purpose. The Bible gives us accounts of God's plans prevailing in the case of Jesus' birth being foretold and fulfilled. Both Micah (5:2) and Isaiah (7:14) prophesied about Jesus' birth. Though they lived in Galilee, Joseph and Mary traveled to Joseph's ancestral home of Bethlehem, Judah as a result of the Roman census just before Jesus was born. There, the virgin Mary gave birth to the Messiah (see Luke 2:1-7). Born in Bethlehem and raised in Galilee, the Son of Man was known as Jesus of Nazareth (see Matthew 2:19-23). All of these events and circumstances were orchestrated in advance by God according to His plan for the birth of His Son.

Like He did with Joseph, Mary, and Jesus, God longs to reveal to you and manifest His wonderful plan for your life. In God's divine time, He will reveal His plan. His ways are not our ways. While we have a limited view of our circumstances, God has an aerial view, an unlimited perspective, and a perfect plan. He providentially orders each element of His plan for your success. God does not do anything haphazardly. Every plan of His is predetermined and meticulously carried out at the right time. In the fullness of time, God will execute each part of His plan for your life (Psalms 31:15) as you pursue the purpose He created you for. Are you answering the call? If not, how could you position yourself to pursue purpose? What makes you peculiar? What are your unique gifts? How are you stewarding your gifts, talents, skills, and knowledge?

How To Use This Book

There are two questions to keep at the forefront of your mind as you embark on this adventure of pursuing purpose: 1) What is God's purpose for your life? 2) Are you pursuing it?

CHAPTER 1

Graced for Success

Grace is the overflowing favor of God, and you can always count on it being available to draw upon as needed.

Oswald Chambers

More than anyone who has ever known you, God is fully aware of your strengths and challenges because He carefully gifted you. In other words, He equipped you with natural abilities (assets and talents) known as gifts to fulfill the purpose He created you for (1 Corinthians 12:11). Not only did God gift you according to His will, He also graced you for your purpose (1 Peter 4:10; Romans 12:6).

Grace, as defined by Bishop Parnell M. Lovelace Jr., is "all of God's power and ability released to and through the believer. It is God extending who He is and what He has through you." In other words, it is the divine empowerment to operate in your gifts. Grace is God's courteous goodwill, intervention, and support that enables you to do what He called you to do. God would never call you to do something that He did not give you the gifts and grace to accomplish. God will always grant grace for your place. When you are where He places you, you will be empowered and supported to do a job with joy that others may dread. Why? Because His grace is sufficient for you (2 Corinthians 12:9).

Because He gifted you, He knows your assets and liabilities, and His power is made perfect in your weakness (2 Corinthians 12:9). It is not one's weaknesses that cause problems, but one's unwillingness to recognize and acknowledge them. It is wise to daily ask God for and rely on His help. Allow Him to intervene—every day and in every circumstance. Remember that you are equipped by His grace (Ephesians 4:7). This fact, when fully comprehended, provides perhaps the greatest sigh of relief for those of us who feel that we are inadequate to accomplish the purposes for which God created us. The truth is: It is God who works in you to act according to His good purpose (Philippians 2:13).

In Matthew 11:30 (NIV), Jesus declared, "For my yoke is easy and my burden is light." Jesus' yoke and burden refer to everything He requires of you. His purpose for your life and the enterprises He wants you to engage in are not burdensome. Instead, they will accompany peace and comfort and will be uplifting. It should be a joy to do what God called you to do. You should thrive in fulfilling your purpose.

When you use your gifts to answer His call, His grace will enable you to operate with ease. That means if you will obediently do what God asks you to do, He will graciously do what only He can do. That doesn't mean there won't be any challenges or that it won't take any undertaking on your part. But what it does mean is that you will experience divine intervention as you engage in the work He equipped you for. Your gifts will artlessly manifest and spurt from you. According to Isaiah 54:17 (NIV), "no weapon forged against you will prevail." He did not say there wouldn't be a weapon, but He promises it won't prosper. So, expect challenges and opposition as you pursue your purpose, but know that His grace is sufficient for you.

Satan will always attempt to frustrate your purpose. The Word of God tells us that a little Hebrew boy, Moses, had a purpose to deliver Israel from 430 years of bondage and slavery in Egypt. But long before he led Israel, he was reared in an Egyptian family as the grandson of Pharaoh while being taught and nurtured by his biological mother who tutored him in the Hebrew religion (see Exodus 2).

After becoming a young man, Moses had to navigate two identities: a double consciousness of being a privileged son raised in the Egyptian king's house and being a Hebrew seeing other Hebrews enslaved to and mistreated by Egyptians. Although he was the Prince of Egypt, Moses was dismayed by the way the Egyptians treated the Israelites. When he was 40 years old, Moses killed an Egyptian for being cruel toward an Israelite slave and buried his body in the sand. The next time Moses attempted to counsel two Hebrews, one asked, "Do you intend to kill me like you killed the Egyptian?" (Exodus 2:14, Amplified Bible). He recognized that his action was not a secret coupled with the fact that the people whom he was born to deliver were not ready for him. So, he fled to Midian, where he led a new life as a shepherd. So much of what Moses experienced as a shepherd in the desert was in stark contrast to being an Egyptian Prince, but there was a purpose in it.

Four decades later, after fleeing to Midian because of his plan being frustrated, Moses returned to Egypt (see Exodus 4) where he was constantly opposed by the Israelites—the people he was born to deliver from bondage. Although Moses, a verbally impaired 80-year-old shepherd, didn't know how to bring to fruition that for which he was born—to liberate a nation, he knew God well enough that he was confident his purpose would be fulfilled.

Though few will be given a task on the scale of Moses', the Father has a purpose for everyone as well as the grace to fulfill it.

Whether that purpose is to raise a godly family, be a witness in the marketplace, or be an entrepreneur, God's plan is for each person to do so in His power. Even though you have grace to attain your purpose, there will always be opposition that will attempt to frustrate or defeat your endeavors. However, when the enemy attempts to frustrate your purpose by inducing feelings of discouragement, you must draw from your reservoir of spiritual strength in order to bounce back like Moses. Know that God will always equip and empower you to fulfill your purpose.

Will you, today, bask in the truth that His yoke is easy, and His burden is light (Matthew 11:30)? If you are engaging in a task that is strenuous and draining, you should pray and ask God for wisdom and discernment regarding your purpose and gifts. You will recognize God's will because His grace will empower and support you and you will be able to engage in all of your endeavors with ease. Let no one frustrate your purpose!

CHAPTER 2

Discerning God's Will: Praying with Purpose

Life's battles are won or lost in the place of prayer.

Charles Stanley

God has a divine plan, and within that plan is a specific purpose for your life. People who live according to the patterns of the world do things in their own strength according to their knowledge. Rather than fulfilling their God-given purposes, they choose to chart their own courses throughout life in pursuit of self-interest, self-advancement, and human reasoning, all of which usually lead to feeling empty and vain (Ecclesiastes 1:14). However, God's wisdom causes us to acknowledge Him in all of our ways and trust that He has our best in mind. "It is God's privilege to conceal things and the king's privilege to discover them." (Proverbs 25:2, NLT). As the One who created us and always knows what is in our best interest, God is committed to accomplishing His good, acceptable, and perfect will (Romans 12:1) through us, but we must seek Him to obtain revelation each step along the way. Prayer and scripture are the two most powerful resources for discerning God's will for your life.

The Power of Prayer

Prayer brings us into an intimate time with God. As you spend quality time with Him, He will reveal information to you. Deuteronomy 29:29 (NIV) says, "the secret things belong to the Lord our God, but the things revealed belong to us...." This means that God knows things that no one else knows. (After all, He is omniscient). He knows what He's doing even when we don't. But, when we draw closer to Him through prayer, He will reveal His will to us. Jesus talked about this, and the apostle John recorded it:

> "I no longer call you servants, because a servant does not know his master's business. Instead, I have called you friends, for everything that I learned from my Father I have made known to you."
>
> John 15:15 (NIV)

The Lord is not secretive. Since we are His friends, Jesus reveals to us what the Father shares with Him (John 15:1,15). He wants to commune with you and show you things you've never seen, heard, or even perceived. The more you enter into the presence of God, the more of His plan you will be privy to, and the more you will experience His best for your life.

The more you get to know the Father, the more you can understand and pray according to His will—His purpose and plan—and the more you will love Him. That is because knowing who He is equates to knowing His desires for you and understanding how He perceives things. When we pray according to His will, God acts according to our petitions. What is truly amazing is that you have unlimited access to God and the privilege of approaching God with your concerns (Hebrews 4:16). Not only will He reveal His will to you, He will also empower you to pursue your purpose in a manner pleasing to Him.

Prioritize Prayer

Prayer must be a top priority. Paul told the Colossians to be devoted to prayer (Colossians 4:2). Prayer should not be viewed as an onerous burden, but as an awesome opportunity to intimately connect with and hear from the Lord concerning His plan for your life, particularly as it pertains to the unique opportunities, tasks, and circumstances set before you. You should always seek God's will above all else. Prioritize His desires above your own. Prayer is the optimum way to do this as the Lord is always willing to speak to you and provide clarity of purpose and directives through this communication process.

In the Bible, we read that Daniel prayed three times daily (Daniel 6:10). Daniel sought God even in mundane times. Even when it was against the law to pray to the God of Israel, Daniel faithfully sought the Lord. In fact, it was Daniel's prioritization of prayer that spurred his jealous colleagues to convince the king to institute a law that would make Daniel's praying to His God illegal (see Daniel 6). Despite being thrown into a den of lions overnight, Daniel trusted God to protect him because he knew Him through conversing with Him multiple times each day. Inspired by Daniel remaining unharmed despite staying overnight in the lions' den, the king instituted a new law requiring all to obey Daniel's God. It was Daniel's prioritization of prayer that led to God being recognized and glorified throughout the Babylonian kingdom.

When instructing His disciples concerning prayer, Jesus said, "When you pray" (Matthew 6:5-6, NIV)—not if you pray. The use of "when" shows that prayer is an expectation for followers of Christ. Prayer is simply speaking with God. "The Lord is near to all who call on Him, to all who call on Him in truth. He fulfills the desires of those who fear Him; He hears their cry and saves them.", wrote King David (Psalm 145:18-19, NIV). In other words, when we pray, God hears us and intervenes on our behalf. Nothing is too big nor too small to consult God about. The Lord delights in His children seeking Him, especially when it pertains to discovering what He wants to do in our lives. He wants you to consult Him with your concerns. He is concerned and wants to be involved in every detail of your life. So, don't just seek Him concerning grand decisions nor wait until a crisis occurs.

Further speaking to the disciples, Jesus promised, "Whatever you ask in my name, this I will do, that the Father may be glorified in the Son." (John 14:13, ESV). While Jesus promises to provide whatever we ask in His name, it is important to realize that prayer is not a magic charm, and God is not a genie we can manipulate to get whatever we want. So, what does it mean to ask in Jesus' name?

I used to think that saying "in Jesus' name" at the end of my petitions validated my prayers. However, saying that phrase is not a prerequisite for God to hear and respond. Instead, praying in Jesus' name means praying according to God's will. When you make requests to the Father that align with His will in Jesus' name, they will be granted and fulfill your joy. Praying in Jesus' name means tapping into an endless power source relinquishing our desires and committing to follow God's plan, which honors Him.

When we pray according to His will, we align our hearts with His and submit to His desires for us. Then, He gives us the desires of our hearts which are in sync with what He wants for us. Like Jesus' first followers, we are His ambassadors living according to God's plan and under His authority. So, whatever we ask for according to His plan will be manifested because it has been His will all along. We just need to align with it, and we demonstrate our alignment by praying according to His plan for our lives.

Using the Word as the source for your requests is the key to praying according to God's will. I am sure you have either heard or said The Lord's Prayer (Matthew 6:9-13). With it, Jesus modeled for His followers what it means to pray according to God's will by stating, "your kingdom come, your will be done, on earth as it is in heaven" (Matthew 6:10, NIV). Praying the Lord's prayer is a great way to make requests according to scripture.

Decades prior to Jesus providing a pattern for prayer to His disciples, Daniel modeled how to pray according to scripture (see Daniel 9). While engrossed in scriptures, Daniel studied Jeremiah's prophecies (see Jeremiah 25:11-12) and discovered that God promised to deliver displaced Israelites from Babylonian captivity after 70 years. With his faith encouraged by the Word, Daniel reminded God that God's reputation was on the line to fulfill His promise.

Scripture lets us know that Daniel prayed at the time of the evening sacrifice, or three o'clock in the evening, for God to rescue the Israelites from Babylon. What is significant about this is not only that God delivered the Israelites from Babylonian captivity, but that centuries later, at the same time—three o'clock in the evening, Jesus died to deliver *all humanity* from sin's captivity. Like Daniel, allow the Word to encourage your faith and choose to pray and put God's reputation on the line, knowing that He is faithful to fulfill His promises. Keep in mind that like Daniel's, your prayer has both short-term and long-term impacts.

Scripture is the basis for effective prayer because it reveals who God is, what He desires, and what He promises to you. Understanding these aspects helps you submit to and pray according to His will for your life. God's Word is essential for recognizing His voice and following Him. Familiarizing yourself with it deepens your relationship with God and provides meaning for pursuing purpose as you are able to perceive life from His perspective.

Meditation

While prayer involves speaking to God, meditation involves listening to Him. Meditation enhances or maintains your ability to acquire and retain information that God reveals to you. In Hebrew, *hagah,* or meditation, means to mutter or speak quietly; to imagine, to study, and to utter (Vine, 1996). It means to reflect with the intent of focusing your thinking. To meditate is to remain in a condition, place, or relationship, or to maintain a particular posture. As believers, meditation positions us to constantly receive what God reveals to us as we spend time with Him.

Throughout the Psalms, especially Chapter 119 (the longest scripture in the Bible), King David mentions meditating upon God's precepts (vv. 15,18), law (v. 97), commands (vv. 48, 98), and statues (v.99), all of which are synonymous with His word, or the Bible. In Psalms 119, King David reveals that God's word is a life compass for fulfilling purpose. To experience life the way God intends for us, we must meditate upon the word. Biblical meditation involves honing in and reflecting upon the word of God in order to apply it to your life.

One of the things I love most about the Bible is its beautiful use of figurative language to illustrate its application to our lives. Psalms 1:1-3 illustrates the importance of meditation as it pertains to fruitful living.

> Blessed is the man that walketh not in the counsel of the ungodly, nor standeth in the way of sinners, nor sitteth in the seat of the scornful. But his delight is in the law of the Lord; and in His law doth he meditate day and night. And he shall be like a tree planted by the rivers of water, that bringeth forth his fruit in his season; his leaf also shall not wither; and whatsoever he doeth shall prosper.
>
> Psalm 1:2-3 (KJV)

Meditation is a great discipline to include in your daily regimen. How often should you meditate? To meditate effectively, you must be consistent and obedient to God in every aspect of your life. In other words, you can't just glance at scripture occasionally or occasionally pray and obey. Don't just do so out of religious obligation, but reverently engage in these disciplines. Effective meditation is a wholehearted effort to know God more intimately in order to pursue the purpose He created you for.

Scripture shows that people who find personal pleasure in consistently and carefully thinking about and applying God's word are blessed. They, like trees planted by water, thrive in all their endeavors. Be encouraged and know that consistently focusing on the word will yield a harvest in your life. Determine in your heart to daily meditate upon the word of God and pray without ceasing, and you will gradually develop wisdom as God gives you His perspective and discernment to guide your decision-making. (To learn more about wisdom and discernment, see Chapter 3). The end result of scripture meditation and application is that we become "equipped for every good work" He established for us (2 Timothy 3:17, NIV).

The Holy Spirit and His Leading

While in biblical times, God spoke to His children through prophets, Hebrews 1:2 tells us that in these last days, He speaks to us through His Son, which is His Word *(John 1:1, 14).* The Son communicates with us through His spirit. The Bible says, "Now the Spirit speaks expressly" (1 Timothy 4:1, AKJV), which means that His spirit—a member of the Trinity—emphasizes the Father's will and purposes to us. As In Touch Ministries beautifully explains in its devotional *Live According to the Spirit,* "The Holy Spirit is a person whom we can know intimately and who continually works to transform us into Christ's image....and will reveal Himself to us through the Scriptures." (In Touch Ministries, 2019b).

When we read and meditate upon scripture, the Holy Spirit Illuminates its meaning and helps us understand and apply it to align with God's will. It is the Holy Spirit who causes reading scripture to be a revelatory and transformational experience rather than a mere academic endeavor. It is the interpreting power of the Holy Spirit that provides supernatural empowerment and enlightenment for applying scripture to precisely pursue purpose.

Understanding scripture helps you see circumstances from God's viewpoint and perceive His plans and purpose for your life. This is known as spiritual discernment—a supernatural ability to make decisions and evaluative judgments beyond information based on our natural senses. We are urged by scripture to set our minds on things above (Colossians 3:2). This means we must change our position from which we naturally view circumstances. We must view things through the lens of the word, not the lens of the world. Scripture teaches that we are seated with Christ in heavenly places (Ephesians 2:6). So, we're not under the circumstances nor equal to the circumstances that we encounter.

Pastor EB Herman paints a more vivid picture:

"You have to refocus. You have to see yourself far above all principalities, all powers, over all the strategies of the enemy. When you see yourself from that position, it'll change your perspective. When you look at things differently, the things you look at will ultimately begin to change, and you start to reset. You start to change the way you are perceiving information."

Commit to knowing God more intimately through His Word, and as you spend time with Him in scripture and prayer, you'll discover, pursue, and fulfill the purpose He created you for.

CHAPTER 3

Seek Spiritual Discernment

Behind everything God does there is a divine purpose. Sometimes it is clear and sometimes it is mysterious. But one thing is certain: He has made His purpose very clear in giving us the Bible.

In Touch Ministries

A significant life is marked by being patterned after God's plan and walking in His ways moment by moment and precept upon precept. This discipline requires discernment, or the ability to judge well or obtain spiritual guidance and understanding. Discernment also refers to insight regarding someone or something despite difficulty by sight or with the other senses. In other words, when you have discernment, you are able to understand or distinguish between people, objects, and good and evil in order to make a decision from God's point of view, even when you are not aware of all the details. Discernment also helps you distinguish between a "good" thing and a "God" thing in order to make the best decision.

Discernment is spiritual insight, which is not based on natural intellect. Paul plainly states, "Who can know the mind of the Lord?...we have the mind of Christ." (1 Corinthians 2:16, NIV). In 1 Corinthians (2:10-12, 16), Paul alludes to the inability of human intellect to discern spiritual matters apart from the divine illumination available only through the Holy Spirit—the inner voice of truth given to all believers. It is the Holy Spirit—our Helper—who illuminates truth to us, for the natural person cannot understand spiritual insights which come from God because they are discerned only through the spirit (John 14:26). However, the person led by God's Spirit is able to judge all things because s(he) is not limited to human intelligence (1 Corinthians 2:14-15). According to Isaiah 55:9 (NIV), "As the heavens are higher than the earth, so are my ways higher than your ways and my thoughts than your thoughts.", declares the Lord. As believers, we are informed by God who knows all things. Rather than being limited to our human perspectives, we have supernatural senses. A spiritual perspective. The mind of Christ. We listen to and follow Him. His priorities are our priorities.

Discernment and Wisdom

A discerning spirit accompanies wisdom and begins with a humble, teachable attitude. James (1:5) tells us to ask the Father if we lack wisdom. In 1 Kings (3:5-14), King Solomon, the wisest man of his time, exemplifies this for us. He was crowned king of Israel, but did not know how to govern the nation (1 Kings 3:7). Although Solomon was God's chosen servant, he realized that he lacked discernment for leading Israel. So, he asked for a discerning heart to govern and distinguish between right and wrong (1 Kings 3:9).

This is a very familiar story. We know that God was so pleased with Solomon's request that He granted him much more than he requested. Not only did God grant Solomon discernment for administering justice, He also lavished upon him wealth and longevity. Notice that God endowed Solomon with a wise and discerning heart. In other words, God accorded Solomon both knowledge and good judgment to make the best decisions in matters set before him. So, not only did Solomon acquire knowledge by facts presented to him, he also received spiritual guidance to perceive beyond the knowledge provided to him in order to exact keen judgment and make the best decisions. God also assured Solomon that longevity would accompany obedience for him (1 Kings 3:14). This implies that although one may have wisdom and the ability to discern between good and evil, (s)he still has to decide to obey God (See Chapter 4 about obedience).

I love that Solomon asked for the ability to discern between good and evil. This may seem miniscule. However, this is often a challenge for everyone. We do not know the motives of others. We can be so easily deceived, but it is the Holy Spirit—our inner teacher—who provides discernment to help us make the best decisions in our relationships, careers, and daily endeavors. As can be seen from the story of Solomon, only God gives divine wisdom, knowledge, and understanding.

Education is no substitute for the wisdom God gives. We need education (knowledge of God's word), but we also need revelation (understanding of God's will). During the Feast of Booths, when Jesus taught in the temple, the Jews marveled saying, "How is it that this man has learning, when he has never studied?" (John 7:15, ESV). His audience marveled because during that time, only Jews who were educated through many years of training at the temple were equipped to teach the law. Educated Jews who received formal religious education also exercised power over the uneducated Jews.

The irony of this scenario is that Jews who received formal religious education in the accepted interpretations of the scriptures were being taught by Jesus who did not undergo formal training.

Not only did He teach the educated Jews by revealing the true meaning of scripture, He made it available to all—including the poor uneducated Jews who could not afford formal education.

Acknowledging the congregation's question, Jesus answered them, "My teaching is not mine, but His who sent me." (John 7:15-16, ESV). Jesus knew that wisdom and revelation only come from God. He also knew how to apply the knowledge that God provided, which enabled Him to reveal the meaning and application of the word to others (Proverbs 22:17-19).

Knowledge is the collection of information conveyed, understanding is the correct interpretation of knowledge, and wisdom is the appropriate application of knowledge. Knowledge can naturally mature into understanding, but wisdom can only come from God. Knowing, understanding, and applying biblical principles are essential for successfully living the life that God intends for you.

There are so many people who, like the Jews who studied for years at the temple, have knowledge and maybe even understanding, but do not possess wisdom. The Bible acknowledges wisdom as the principal thing. Why? Because it is operational insight, or the ability to look beyond what is conveyed and know what to do. In other words, wisdom is of supreme importance because unlike knowledge and understanding, wisdom only comes from God, and it accompanies discernment—insight beyond one's limited carnal perspective. Only God can empower you with wisdom, or the ability to apply knowledge to make the best decisions beyond your natural comprehension.

Wisdom is the ability to view things from God's perspective and apply godly principles for decision-making. God does not want us to make decisions based on mere appearance or human reasoning. He wants us to be wise.

King Solomon once wrote, "Happy (blessed, fortunate, enviable) is the man who finds skillful *and* godly wisdom, and the man who gets understanding [drawing it forth from God's Word and life's experiences]." (Proverbs 3:13, AMPC). The Bible gives us examples of situations in which needs arose for someone with godly wisdom to interpret events that occurred, and in each case, only those who reverenced God were able to interpret events and were abundantly blessed as a result of it. That is because "the fear of the Lord is the beginning of wisdom, and the knowledge of the Holy One is insight." (Proverbs 9:10, ESV).

When King Belshazzar wanted to know the interpretation of the writing on the wall, the queen told him to summon Daniel as he was known as a godly man with a wise spirit (see Daniel 5). As a result of exercising wisdom to reveal the mystery, Daniel was rewarded with royal clothing and kingdom rulership. The Bible also gives us an account of Joseph, a man of integrity and wisdom, being summoned while in prison to interpret Pharaoh's dream (see Genesis 41). After interpreting Pharaoh's dream, which resulted in Egypt surviving a devastating famine, Joseph was given royal clothing and the king's signet ring and leadership over Egypt. Proverbs promises that wisdom accompanies valuable benefits such as favor, wealth, longevity, and advancement, as can be seen from the examples of Daniel and Joseph. It is the same in your life. When you pursue and exercise wisdom, you will experience abundant blessing upon everything you set out to do.

Wisdom only comes from knowing God and understanding what His will is for us, being in His will, and desiring to remain in it. John 10:27 (ESV) says, "My sheep hear my voice, and I know them, and they follow me." How do we know Him? By knowing His word. Knowing His word equates to Knowing His will, and knowing His will leads to obedience. Knowing and understanding God's Word increases our ability to discern His leading. Having the Holy Spirit is the beginning of spiritual discernment, but obeying Him is critical for experiencing the benefits of spiritual discernment.

Always embrace and retain the wisdom of God, for there will come a time in your life in which circumstances are designed to require revelation from God. Like Daniel and Joseph, if you revere God and seek His insight, He can use you to solve significant problems and bring glory to Him.

Today, ask God to reveal the secret things to you. Then, allow the Holy Spirit to show you what you are unable to perceive with your natural senses, and He will give you the right perspective. He will do it if you ask, for His word promises that our generous Father will give you wisdom and will not rebuke you for asking (James 1:5).

What Is Your Purpose?

Ephesians is a book that shares principles of purpose, and the writer, Paul, devotes substantial time showing us that our heavenly Father predestined us to become His children which he purposed through Christ to unify heaven and earth under Him (Ephesians 1:4-5; 10-11). This lets us know that pursuing purpose begins with salvation—a one-time event, but it also involves ongoing activity.

While Jesus knew that He came to earth to fulfill the Father's ultimate redemption plan by dying in lieu of corrupt people to save humanity from sin (John 3:16), He did not decide to live idly by just waiting to die at 33.5 years old. Instead, He said, "I must be about my Father's business" (Luke 2:49, KJV) as He engaged in the works [e.g. teaching (see Matthew 5), healing (see Matthew 8:16; 12:15), befriending sinners (see Luke 19:1-10)], and etcetera the Father planned for Him to do prior to His crucifixion. Jesus said, "...whoever believes in me will do the works I have been doing, and they will do even greater things than these..." (John 14:12, NIV). As you can see, purpose encompasses God-given works. On the contrary, pursuing anything apart from God will prove to be empty and disappointing.

I think it is safe to say that there are many people in the world who are unaware of their God-given purposes, and they are seeking advice from webinars, podcasts, TED Talks, and life coaches, as well as fulfillment in different occupations. The enemy desires for people to search for answers from all other sources than the One who created the purpose for which they exist. He wants people to seek fulfillment in their occupations rather than seek God's will. The most exciting thing about purpose is that it can be fulfilled with any occupation (whether faith-based or not). It is not limited to clergy. So, whether you have a job you like or decide to change jobs, whether you read a book, attend a webinar, or subscribe to a podcast, be sure to not neglect your purpose while doing so. Know that you exist to be subject to God's authority, and that He providentially weaves the threads of His call throughout your life to fulfill His will.

To identify and understand your purpose, you should ask God and search the scriptures in every aspect of your life. As you seek Him through prayer and the Word, He will work in your heart and mind to guide you and develop your discernment. Hebrews 4:12 (NIV) says, "For the word of God is alive and active. Sharper than any double-edged sword, it penetrates even to dividing soul and spirit, joints and marrow; it judges the thoughts and attitudes of the heart." Knowing the word of God will sharpen your discernment. The more you read, understand, and study the Bible, the more you will know God and His plan for you. According to John 1:1(NIV), "In the beginning was the Word, and the Word was with God, and the Word was God." God is the word. So, when you learn the word, you learn God. You learn what He (dis)likes, loves, and abhors. The more you have the word of God inside of you, the better you will be able to perceive His will, plan, and purpose for your life.

God speaks clearly to and answers the prayers of anyone who meditates upon scripture and abides in Him. He wants to intimately communicate with you by speaking to your heart, but you must listen by meditating upon His word. You should read scripture prayerfully and frequently and ask the Holy Spirit to enlighten your understanding of the Father's commands. Ask Him to illuminate the scriptures to you. Trust that as the greatest Helper and Teacher, He will guide you into the truth of scripture and speak to you through the passages. While reading and praying, be sure to note observations and ask questions. Ask the Holy Spirit to help you apply the word to your life. Know that He will provide divine guidance each step of the journey to help you walk in His will. As you prayerfully read scripture and seek God's will for your life, you will constantly hear from God and receive His directives for pursuing your purpose.

Scripture constantly reminds us to "pray without ceasing" (1 Thessalonians 5:16, ESV). I urge you to consult God about everything. Do not view prayer as a duty to perform, but as an opportunity to invite God to direct every area of your life. Praying and hearing from God should be something you anticipate and enjoy doing.

God has given us access to the Holy Spirit's wisdom and discernment to ensure alignment with His will while pursuing purpose. It is the Holy Spirit that will help you examine your desires and ensure that they are driven by godly ambition. When you lean on the Holy Spirit, you allow Him to dictate your desires, which will be compatible with your calling.

Are there any unshakable dreams in your heart? Do you meditate on any promises from God regarding your future? If God made the promise, He will manifest it. He would not place a dream in your heart without providing what you need to accomplish it. Hold on to the desires God placed in your heart. If He put them there, He will fulfill them. If He gave you the dream, He graced you to fulfill it. Know that He has every intention of bringing it to pass. When your objectives match His, you will pursue the purpose He predestined you for. Not only did He place the desire within your heart, He will also work with you and through you to manifest it.

What is the Lord calling you to do? This can be discerned with knowledge the Holy Spirit imparts to you. A couple of ways you can identify your purpose is by taking a spiritual gifts assessment and self-reflecting to examine what you enjoy most (see Appendix). What are your hobbies, gifts, and talents? What could you envision yourself doing, even if you did not get paid to do so? When you have a definite purpose, you understand why it matters and can develop clear goals for pursuing it (see Chapter 5).

One clear goal each person should have is to live for God by pursuing the purpose for which (s)he was created. When you have clear goals, like Jesus, you will not just go through the motions. Instead, you will be intentional in pursuing your purpose.

CHAPTER 4

The Blessing of Obedience

The fastest way to get to the life of your dreams is to obey God.

Francis Anfuso

All of God's intentions (Jeremiah 29:11; 1 Corinthians 2:9) toward you far exceed your expectations (Ephesians 3:20), but you must obey Him in order to fulfill His customized plan for your life. Obedience is compliance to an order, request, or law, or submission to another's authority (Oxford University Press, 2022a). Obeying God requires compliance to His plan and yielding to His purpose for your life. It means committing to follow Him despite the consequences. Simply put, to obey God means to do what He called you to do. This involves not only accomplishing what He desires, but aligning with His instructions and timing.

Throughout our lives, God provides countless opportunities to obey Him. Why? Because obedience is the pathway to wisdom and blessing. In Deuteronomy (28:2), the Word of God promises that blessings overtake those who obey the voice of the Lord. Jesus made obedience to the Father's will the supreme priority of His life. In the previous chapter, we looked at wisdom and how Jesus, who received no formal training, taught those who did receive formal training by the wisdom He received from the Father. Now, we will look at examples of blessings that accompanied obedience.

What does it mean to be blessed? The Hebrew word for blessed is *barak*, which signifies life and prosperity (Butler, 2017). Being blessed refers to God's empowerment and favor as a result of conforming to His will. Being blessed is all about fully embracing your calling and receiving all that God has for you. This encompasses longevity and success. Being blessed begins with obedience.

Sometimes obeying God may require simple actions, while at other times, big acts of obedience may be required, both of which could seem ludicrous. A man named Naaman in 2 Kings Chapter 5 is a wonderful example of someone whose small step of obedience resulted in a significant blessing. He was a commander and a mighty man of valor of the Syrian army, but he was a leper. Informed of the prophet Elisha in Samaria by Naaman's wife's maid—a little girl from Israel, Naaman went to see Elisha to be healed of leprosy. When Naaman arrived at Elisha's house, Elisha did not personally greet him. Instead, he sent instructions for him to go and wash in the Jordan River seven times to be healed.

Much to Naaman's chagrin, Elisha did not approach Naaman and pray for him. Instead, he sent a messenger to instruct him to wash at a river that did not have the cleanest water in the region. So, he angrily departed scorning Elisha's command. Perhaps being a man of great stature who was highly favored by the Syrian king, Naaman was accustomed to and expected an elaborate greeting and royal treatment from Elisha. But Naaman's servants said to him, "My father, if the prophet had bid you to do some great thing, would you not have done it?" (2 Kings 5:13, AMPC). So, he decided to obey, and as a result, he was cured of leprosy.

God was not trying to embarrass Naaman. Instead, He chose Naaman's desperate circumstance to prove His ability to heal him in an unconventional way. The Jordan River was not the most exquisite, but it is where God decided to heal Naaman. In the same way in our lives, God's motive is always pure. His desire is always intended to bless us, whether that be in the form of healing or other types of victory. If we will release our cares to Him and expectations of how we think He should intervene in our circumstances, we will experience His power in our lives in mighty ways.

Oftentimes, God will turn small ordinary steps of obedience into great extraordinary blessings.

The Benefits of Obedience

Your blessing is on the other side of your obedience. In John chapter 9, Jesus and His disciples saw a blind man. The disciples assumed the man's blindness was a result of his or his parents' sin. However, instead of viewing the man's blindness as a result of sin, Jesus saw it as an opportunity for God to heal him and be glorified. After seeing the man who was born blind, Jesus put His saliva on the man's eyes and told him to go wash in the pool of Siloam. Obeying Jesus' command, the man was able to see. Sometimes the Lord instructs us to do things that confound human reasoning and defy logic, but obeying Him always results in a blessing.

Because the formerly blind man obeyed Jesus' instructions, he received both physical and spiritual sight. This man's obedience resulted in the opening of his eyes and his heart to accept and worship Christ, thus glorifying God. Through the formerly blind man's obedience, Jesus transformed his life. Like this man, your obedience to the Lord will always prove Him to be trustworthy. Do not take

Naaman's initial disposition and allow pride to keep you from obeying God. Instead, be like the formerly blind man by immediately following His instructions for your life and keeping your eyes fixed on Jesus, knowing that He is trustworthy.

We must not lean on our own understanding (Proverbs 3:5), but obey God even when it does not make sense. The Apostle Peter made a seemingly absurd decision when He relinquished his profession to accept Jesus' invitation to be His disciple (see Matthew 4:18-20). But through his obedience, Peter embarked upon a life-changing journey and became one of the greatest and most effective apostles who contributed significantly to establishing the church. Likewise, God can use you in powerful ways to accomplish His will, but you must be obedient.

In Joshua chapters 3-5, after Moses died, the Lord told Joshua to prepare to cross the Jordan River to acquire new territory that He would give the Israelites. God also told Joshua that no one would successfully oppose Him the rest of his life. Although God presented Joshua with a command and a promise, Joshua still had to obey God and boldly lead the Israelites to cross the Jordan River. So, Joshua instructed, and the Israelites obeyed all that God told Moses (before he died) and Joshua as they prepared to cross the Jordan and possess the Promised Land God was giving them.

Obeying the Lord, the priests carrying the ark of the covenant approached the Jordan river ahead of the rest of the Israelites, and all of Israel crossed the river on dry ground as a result of it. Like the Israelites who were led by Joshua, you must be strong, courageous, and obedient to what the Lord has called you to do in order to be successful.

Obeying God often involves risk-taking. A risk is the possibility of suffering loss, danger, or ill will. The ancient Greek writer Herodotus suggests, "Great deeds are usually wrought at great risks." Some of the most potent and memorable examples of taking risks to obey God are found in the Bible. Gideon, a great hero of the Bible, is known as one of the greatest military leaders in scripture. Prior to Gideon becoming a valiant warrior, Israel was taken captive and devastated by Midian for years, and Gideon hid from his enemies. Obeying God's command, though he was fearful and felt ill-equipped, Gideon destroyed an altar of Baal (see Judges 6:28-40) —the pagan idol that was revered in the region where he lived. Risking his life, Gideon, who perceived himself as weak and inadequate, believed God would protect him, and God obliged.

The final event is recorded in Judges 7. Gideon led a grossly outnumbered army of 300 men to deliver Israel from the Midianites who oppressed the Israelites for seven years. Gideon and company pursued and subdued their enemies, and the nation was at rest for the next 40 years under Gideon's leadership. While Gideon was the youngest son in his family, which was the least of its tribe among the Israelites, God called him a "mighty man of valor" and empowered him to lead Israel into victory over its oppressor. But, Gideon's victory began with obeying his calling.

Elsewhere in scripture, we see Esther, a Jewish queen in a Persian empire, who hid her identity to blend in with Persian culture (Esther 2:10). After learning about an evil scheme to annihilate the Jews, Mordecai, Esther's cousin, urged her to reveal her Jewish identity to the king and intercede on behalf of the Jews for him to spare their lives (Esther 4:14-14). Determined to obey despite the consequences, Esther declared a fast among the Jews before appearing before the king with her request (Esther 4:15-17). The Jews' compliance showed their reverence to and reliance upon God to protect them.

From the actions of Mordecai, Esther, and the rest of the Jews in Persia, we eventually see that obedience accompanies favor. Esther risked her life by appearing to the king for a request without being initially summoned to enter his court as well as by pleading for the Jews (see Esther 5:2-3; 7:1-3). Realizing that Esther had a great need when she broke the law, the king offered his scepter to her (Esther 8:4). Because of Esther's actions, the lives of the Jews were spared, while their enemies were killed as a result of the evil plot to exterminate the Jews throughout the Persian kingdom. As a result of their obedience, the Jews witnessed the gracious hand of God as He provided victory for them.

From the lives of Gideon and Esther, we see that obedience accompanies risk-taking. Both of these risk-takers obeyed God and left the consequences to Him. Though himself timid, Gideon was boldly used by God as a result of obeying and trusting in Him. Like Gideon, you may feel inadequate as a result of your circumstances, but God sees you as more than a conqueror (Romans 8:37) because He knows what He can do through you (1 John 4:4) when you obey Him. Though Esther was the last person in her family line, this did not stop her from risking her life to save her people, for she firmly said to Mordecai "If I perish, I perish" (Esther 4:16, NIV), meaning that she would appeal to the king on behalf of the Jews despite the consequences. Like Esther, each of us is called to fulfill a purpose for such a time as this (Esther 4:14). But, fulfilling purpose begins with obedience. When you take risks to obey God, you will experience victory against all odds.

God always assumes full responsibility for the consequences of your obedience. Not only do we see this from Gideon's obedience, the story of Esther also shows how God intervenes to protect us when we obey Him. Although frightened and in need of additional encouragement from the Lord (see Judges 6:36-40), Gideon risked his life by leading an outnumbered army of men to defend Israel against its enemies. After hearing about Haman's (the king's chief advisor) plot to kill the Jews, Esther risked her life to save her nation (see Esther 3, 7). Like Gideon and Esther, we must not limit God nor our obedience to Him by focusing on our circumstances. Instead, we have to obey God and be willing to take risks—no matter what!

Do not analyze your situation from your natural perspective. Your path may not always be clear to you, but He promises to guide you with a steady eye (Psalms 32:8). Your part is to follow in obedience. As can be seen with Gideon, God will often encourage and confirm His will to you when you are walking in obedience (see Judges 6:20-23). Although His commands may seem unreasonable, you can always rely upon His guidance because He is omniscient. His promise is: "... I will be with you; I will never leave you nor forsake you." (Joshua 1:5, NIV). As God promised Joshua, if you meditate on His word daily and obey it, you will be prosperous and successful (Joshua 1:8).

Deuteronomy 28:1-2 (NIV) presents the choice we must make, and it is still the foremost choice for every believer:

> If you fully obey the Lord your God and carefully follow all His commands...., the Lord your God will set you high above all the nations on earth. All these blessings will come upon you and accompany you if you obey the Lord your God.

Of all the advice I could offer you today, the most imperative would be "fully obey the Lord your God and carefully follow all His commands." Remember, obedience is always right. It is the surest path to blessings—life and prosperity. Dare to obey God!

Are you living a life of obedience as exhibited by total submission to His will for your life? What does God want you to do? Are you complying with His commands, or are you disobeying His decrees?

If you ever wonder if you are obeying His commands, check your actions. God graced each of us with a purpose and commanded us to grow in grace and knowledge of Him (2 Peter 3:18). To do this, we must meditate and reflect on the word, renew our minds, confess our sins, and repent of them. We must also apply the word immediately.

Daily devotion (e.g. scriptural reading and study, prayer, quiet time, journaling, etc.) demonstrates values of God's teaching and commands as well as helps us think biblically. When we think biblically, we pattern our behaviors according to God's will. I find that when I invest in uninterrupted daily devotion, I receive spiritual and natural revelations. Scripture commands us to commit our ways unto the Lord, and our thoughts will be established (Proverbs 16:3).

While the Lord may not choose to work within the realm of what seems normal nor always require impressive feats from us, He does expect and honor all acts of obedience—no matter the size of the task. Obeying Him begins with knowing His word. Scripture provides his ever-present commands, makes you wiser (than your enemies), gives insight and understanding, and keeps you from evil.

What are you willing to risk to fulfill the assignment God administered to you? American author Margaret J. Wheatley once said, "Determination, energy, and courage appear spontaneously when we care deeply about something. We take risks that are unimaginable in any other context". Choose to obey God. When you obey God, you are never a victim of your circumstance, but always a victor! You have His overcoming power because "greater is He in you than He who is in the world." (1 John 4:4, NASB). With Him, you always triumph!

CHAPTER 5

What Is Your Vision?

Write down the revelation and make it plain...
Habakkuk 2:2a (NIV)

Your calling, or purpose, could be fulfilled within your occupation or the profession you are pursuing. However, you should never equate nor limit your purpose to your profession, for purpose and profession are two different things. Your purpose is to glorify God and edify others by reflecting His heart and image through your lifestyle. Purpose, unlike profession, does not change. It encompasses all of the "good works God prepared beforehand" for you to accomplish (Ephesians 2:10). Your profession, on the other hand, is an avenue to earn a living, help people, and solve problems. Pursuing purpose and/or a profession is not a haphazard ordeal. If you pursue or are currently engaged in a profession, chances are you envisioned being in that role countless times before acquiring the position.

Purpose enacts vision. I feel it is important to dedicate a chapter in this book to the concept of vision which, like purpose, requires intentionality.

Vision is the ability to think about or plan the future with imagination or wisdom. One of the keys to your dreams coming to pass is to imagine them manifested before they exist. Albert Einstein once said, "Imagination is everything. It is the preview of life's coming attractions." Einstein knew that seeing is believing. If you can see it through the eyes of faith, you will eventually attain it.

It all starts with mentally envisioning the manifestation of your vision. Ideas are produced from imagination. Imagination is where dreams are formed. It is where inspiration is received and added to experience to influence action. The development and use of your imagination influences your limitations or lack thereof. Pastor EB Herman says, "if something is too big for your mind, it's too big for your hand." In other words, you can't produce what you can't perceive. However, what you perceive, you can pursue and produce. You will only invest time in what is realistic to you. Submit your vision to the Lord and allow Him to paint the picture of it on the canvas of your mind. Then, focus on fulfilling your vision plan.

Visualizing and focusing on fulfilling your vision will reprogram your subconscious mind to produce future experiences aligned with your purpose. Your subconscious influences your actions and feelings even when you are unaware that it is happening. It is so powerful that although you may be unaware, your conscious mind will always align with how your subconscious mind operates.

You will enact what you envision. This is because your mental images are detected by your subconscious which influences your actions. Mental images are so powerful that they influence your brain to respond to imagined scenarios in the same manner that it would to authentic events. This means that whatever you envision, whether tangible or intangible, you will produce. So, when you set a goal and envision yourself achieving it, your subconscious mind will influence your conscious mind to pursue and attain your desire

(Reddan at al, 2018 as cited in Lee, 2020). Your thoughts will influence your actions.

Before writing this book, I envisioned myself at my book signing taking pictures and signing my autograph. Before I wrote the book, I visualized my picture and biography on the back of the book. I had a picture in my mind of a completed book that I authored. I imagined myself being an author of a book so much so that I began moving toward it. My imagination stirred my passion and motivation to write.

Visualization is the key to unlocking your purpose. Perhaps you can envision an outcome you'd like to see manifest. Could you picture your child graduating? Reconciliation in a relationship? A successful business plan unfold? The key is to visualize it. Then, you will actively pursue it and watch it produce. What are you visualizing? Choose to see your situation with the eyes of faith. Get it in your mind's eye and stay focused on it.

Be Faith-Minded

Most people live solely based upon their physical senses. However, there's more to life than what the physical senses perceive. In fact, everything that pertains to fulfilling one's purpose in life exists in the spiritual realm, but one must first believe it's there. From a physical perspective, this may seem unrealistic, but from a spiritual perspective, this is reality. The mind of the flesh, explained by the Apostle Paul, in Romans 8:6 "is sense and reason without the Holy Spirit", but the mind of the spirit is governed by the Holy Spirit. These mindsets oppose each other (Galatians 5:17, AMPC). If we think with the mind of the flesh, we rely on our own energy, ability, or experience, and we allow our physical senses and circumstances to dictate our actions. Conversely, if we think with the mind of the spirit, we place our expectation in God and allow Him to dictate our thoughts and actions despite our circumstances.

There are things that exist in the spiritual realm but are invisible to the naked eye. Think about the wind and gravity. It is impossible to see them, but you know they exist because you experience the effects of those forces. The same applies spiritually. There are forces that exist within the spiritual realm that we cannot see with our natural eyes, but we can experience their effects. 2 Corinthians 4:18 (KJV) says, "we look not at the things which are seen, but at the things which are not seen." When you navigate with your spiritual senses, you can see things that exist beyond the physical realm. The more you do this, the more you can discern and comprehend what God wants to reveal to you. This type of insight is known as faith, of which God has given to each person a certain amount (Romans 12:3).

Faith is the ability to believe. It is believing God's word under any circumstances (usually despite the circumstances). Faith is the adamant belief that God will perform what He promised. In Matthew 14:29, Jesus told Peter to walk on the water. Before Peter stepped out of the boat and onto the Sea of Galilee, it seemed like a ludicrous thing to do, but he trusted Jesus. From this passage, we see that faith is trusting God no matter how impossible the odds are. You just have to believe and not doubt, and all you need is faith the size of a mustard seed (Matthew 17:20). If God's word said it, and you begin to apply it, by faith, you'll see the manifestation of what it is you're believing for.

Know Your Why—-Passion And Purpose

What are you passionate about? Passion will help you develop a clear vision for pursuing purpose. When you have a clear vision and motive, you have a definite purpose, which multiplies your effort.

You will be intentional and precise in establishing goals and achieving them. You will also maintain focus, high energy, and enthusiasm as you passionately pursue your purpose. A definite purpose and clear vision enable you to do your best work. Your vision drives your passionate pursuit. This keeps you committed, motivated, and focused at an optimal level. Having a clear motive fuels your discipline, effort, and creativity. Passion compels you to fight for your dream with reckless abandon.

Perhaps you've seen the popular video in which comedian Michael Jr. (2015) asks a man in the audience to sing "Amazing Grace", and the man sings a portion of the song twice. While the man sings the song well both times, the second time he sings it is unlike the first because he sings it with a rationale, or a defined purpose for singing. His reason for singing impacts his emotion, intonation, and expression. That is what passion does in your pursuit of purpose. Passion fuels, encourages, excites, gives hope, and propels forward.

A consuming passion encompasses motivation and enthusiasm. Passion is no ordinary desire. Unlike a mere thought that is abstract and of no value, passion is specific, resilient, and determined to be acted upon. Passion is driven by the prefrontal cortex (PFC) of the brain. This is a large and complex region of the brain that plays a pivotal role in decision-making and commanding emotional behaviors (Siddiqui et al., 2008). When you are passionate about pursuing your purpose, your PFC is activated to command continual action in the direction of accomplishing your goals. Being responsible for executive functions such as focusing, planning, organizing, and problem-solving (Petrides et al., 2012), your PFC is driven by your passion to cognitively influence you toward keeping your vision at the forefront of your mind and working toward mastering your goals. When you passionately pursue your purpose, your brain cognitively reinforces your zeal which keeps you motivated and encouraged to work toward achieving your goals.

When you picture fulfilling your vision in your mind's eye, you experience joy, and as a result of your excitement and anticipation, your actions align in the direction of pursuing your vision. What are you believing for? See it in your mind's eye. See yourself fulfilling your purpose. See yourself debt-free. See yourself as a college graduate, an entrepreneur, a homeowner. When you envision your dreams manifested, that vision will move you toward fulfilling your purpose.

While realizing your vision is an incredible gift from God that provides a glimpse of His purpose for your life, you must have clear motives in order to intentionally pursue your purpose. You must also establish goals and a plan for achieving those goals as well as diligently commit to the plan.

Goals

When you have a vision, you need to identify goals that are essential to fulfilling it. Goals are simply desires you aim to accomplish in order to fulfill your vision. Think of goals as the steps along the way, and the vision as the destination. You cannot have a goal without an aim. A goal has an aim and outcome in mind. In other words, your goals are what you desire and work to achieve.

Perhaps you are still trying to determine your vision, and that is okay. Maybe you are experiencing success in your career path, but do not feel as if you are pursuing purpose. Maybe you had a fulfilling career and are now retired, wondering *what's next?* Whether you have a clear vision or not, you should have clear goals. What is something you want to accomplish before the end of this year? What about the end of the month, or the end of the week? Start there. Do you have a planner or calendar? If not, use a sheet of paper or digital instrument to record your goals. It could be a financial goal to save or invest a certain amount of money. It could be a budgeting goal, health and fitness goal, or a traveling goal. It could also be a goal for your family or a relationship. Whatever goals you have, you should clearly identify them and write them down. You should also revisit them at least weekly, if not daily until you accomplish them.

Living, working, or doing anything without identifying goals often involves wasted time and energy. It equates to aiming for nothing while expecting to hit a bull's eye. Accomplishing goals, however, requires clarity. In order to know what you already have as well as what you need to move closer to achieving your goals, you must first clarify your goals. You have to know what you want to do. For example, growing up, I always wanted to be an elementary school teacher. So, throughout grade school and college, I volunteered in elementary classrooms. I also majored in elementary education in order to acquire my degree and teacher certification.

Goal setting directs focus and energy toward accomplishing your God-given purpose. When your goals are established, you know what you need and what you need to do to achieve your objectives. For example, when I set out to write this book, I identified clear goals and made plans to achieve them along the way. My main goal was to write a faith-based inspirational book to encourage individuals to pursue purpose. To achieve this goal, I created deadlines and set aside time to write consistently. Although I did not have to return to school for formal training to learn how to be an author, I did have to expose myself to different writing styles by reading different books and I had to add to my knowledge base about topics covered in this book.

After identifying your goals, you must create a plan for achieving them and you must implement that plan. You must establish realistic deadlines and procedures for meeting them. Developing and implementing your plan is what will transform your intangible desires into the tangible reality you are aiming for. This puts your desire into action. Your plan will lead your actions in the right direction. You should wake up each day recalling your goals and keeping your plan in motion. This will help you manage your time and resources wisely.

Wisdom does in the present what it will be pleased with in the future. Setting goals and outlining a plan will keep you motivated and focused because you know what you want and how to acquire it. Although things may not always happen as you expect, careful planning will prepare you to successfully navigate and execute when the unexpected occurs. On the other hand, failure to plan could force you away from the path of accomplishing your goals when you have to pivot to respond to the unexpected. King Solomon sums up this principle so well when he writes, "Careful planning puts you ahead in the long run; hurry and scurry puts you further behind." (Proverbs 21:5, MSG).

Of course, it takes more than imagination, passion, faith, and goals to see your dreams manifest. Your vision has to align with God's plan, and you have to be prayerful, obedient, and focused to fulfill the purpose He created you for.

CHAPTER 6

Faith In Action (Part 1): Develop A Blueprint

Visualize this thing that you want, see it, feel it, believe in it. Make your mental blueprint, and begin to build.

Robert Collier

Since a vision will not fulfill itself, it would be wise to establish a plan for executing your vision in order to fulfill it. As the French writer Antoine de Saint-Exupéry said, "A goal without a plan is a wish." Developing a plan or blueprint for fulfilling your goals is essential for achieving them.

The words of the physician Luke provide helpful insight pertaining to planning.

> "Suppose one of you wants to build a tower. Won't you first sit down and estimate the cost to see if you have enough money to complete it? For if you lay the foundation and are not able to finish it, everyone who sees it will ridicule you, saying, 'This person began to build and wasn't able to finish.' "
>
> Luke 14:28-30 (NIV)

Before a contractor builds a house, he outlines a blueprint. The blueprint informs the construction company about the materials and resources needed. One does not need building materials to draw the blueprint, but he does need the blueprint to inform him of the resources needed to align with the vision.

Your vision is the foundation of your blueprint which gives meaning and direction to all of your efforts. It is the focal point that all of your endeavors (where you spend your resources—time, money, and effort) should point to. What is your vision for your career, finances, relationships, or other endeavors of importance to you? What are your proximal and distal goals? How do you plan to reach your goals? Answers to these questions can help you design the blueprint for your vision plan.

Prayer-based Planning

Too often, we make plans based on our ideas without seeking God—the master builder—regarding what to do until we get stuck. However, His perfect plan requires no guesswork on our part. God wants to provide clear directives for your blueprint. He wants you to consult Him so He can actively collaborate with you in your design. You just have to ask Him for direction, knowing that "whatever you ask for in prayer and faith is yours." (Mark 11:24, NIV). Praying is the wisest thing you can do in order to design a clear and effective blueprint.

Prayer should always precede planning. Prayer is an invitation for God to enter your situation. Though often taken for granted, it is a remarkable privilege that you are urged to engage in with confidence, knowing that God stands ready to assist you whenever you ask (Hebrews 4:16). Prayer should always be the first action, not the last resort. When you acknowledge God before making decisions, you demonstrate your trust in Him to guide your actions which will always result in the best outcomes. Rather than relying upon your own reasoning, allow Him to reveal the good works He has prepared for you to do (Ephesians 2:10). As the omniscient One, He will help you align the blueprint for your vision with His will. It is important to pray before making decisions.

God knows what you need before you ask. Praying does not guarantee that you will always receive what you request. Even if God does not grant what you request, He will always provide what you need. Oftentimes He may withhold what you think you want because He has something better for you. You just have to seek and trust Him moment by moment, knowing that there is no need too great for Him to meet.

Jesus, in talking to His disciples on the mount, provided the perfect example of this type of disposition. He said:

> "Look at the birds of the sky, that they do not sow, nor reap, nor gather crops into barns, and yet your heavenly Father feeds them. Are you not much more important than they? And which of you by worrying can add a single day to his life's span? And why are you worried about clothing? Notice how the lilies of the field grow; they do not labor nor do they spin thread for cloth.....But seek first His kingdom and His righteousness, and all these things will be provided to you."
>
> Matthew 6:26-28, 33 (NASB)

Prayer helps you prioritize appropriately. Jesus encouraged the disciples not to worry, but instead, to consider the lilies and how they grow. The lilies are not planted. They just spring up from the ground. As lilies grow and are exposed to the sunlight, they open up and flourish. In the same manner, when you expose yourself to the true Source of Light by seeking Him, you will be sensitive to His input regarding your ideas, and He will give life to your blueprint.

The Lord is genuinely interested in what concerns you, and He wants you to live the abundant life He purposed for you. To do so, you must not overlook the essential sequence of priorities and provision Jesus outlines: "Seek first His kingdom and His righteousness, and all these things will be provided to you." (Matthew 6:33, NASB). This requires spending time with God through prayer and scripture while obeying His commands.

Your purpose does not consist in the abundance of things you possess or aim to acquire. Instead, it is inherent in the works God created you to fulfill (Ephesians 2:10). Contrastingly, if you are convinced your purpose is found in external things such as assets, money, status, power, and etcetera, you will attempt to find fulfillment in them. However, chasing after things will only lead to disappointment and vanity overall.

Instead of pursuing materialism, pursue God. If you want God to bless your blueprint, seek His kingdom and righteousness. As you pursue purpose by seeking God, materials will seek after you. Not some things, but ALL things, in Jesus you will find!

Delight yourself in the Lord, and He will give you the desires of your heart (Psalms 37:4). The more you seek Him, the more you become aware of His ways. You also develop discernment to design a blueprint that will withstand all opposition. Choose to allow God to guide you according to His will for you instead of planning first and asking Him to bless the plans you made without consulting Him. Make a commitment to pray instead of taking action without seeking God first. Only then will you align with His plan and experience peace.

Faith and Works

Your actions demonstrate your faith. When you believe something, your actions will show it. Consider biblical models of faith. Believing God's promises, Abraham left his hometown to travel to an unknown place (see Genesis 12). Like Abraham, Ruth left her homeland and resettled in unfamiliar territory (see Ruth 1). Moreover, although Mary was wrongfully accused of immorality, she and Joseph willingly embraced embarrassment, rumors, and hardship to fulfill God's plan of delivering and parenting the promised Messiah (see Matt. 1:18-19; 2:13, 22).

In the same manner, when you believe God, your actions will prove it. What is God asking you to do? Is He challenging you to change something about yourself or your routine? Is He asking you to step outside of your comfort zone? Perhaps He has a different job opportunity or career path for you. To fulfill your highest potential, you must be willing to transition from your "safe zone" to your "faith zone". Remember, God blesses what you do. So, your obedience is what He will reward when you step out on faith.

Writing the vision is an act of faith and obedience. When you put your plan in writing, you develop a blueprint and give a more concrete form to your desires. When you do this, you are saying *"Lord, I don't know how this is going to work out, but I'm writing my vision. I may not have all the resources I need, but I'm writing the vision. I still need to develop a budget to sponsor my plans, but I'm writing the vision."* Friend, you have to give God something to work with. When you write the vision, He will supernaturally work on your behalf to bring it to pass.

The good news is you do not have to have it all figured out. You do not have to know everything because God is omniscient. We know in part and see in part (1 Corinthians 13:9). If you will begin to outline the vision with what you already know, God will provide further insights, and He will place people in your path to come alongside you to help inform your vision. However, it is your vision based on YOUR dreams. So, you must begin to write the vision.

I'm reminded of John 6:5-14. In this passage, thousands of people who gathered to see Jesus were hungry. However, the only food in the area were two fish and five loaves of bread which belonged to a boy. Although Jesus knew what He would do to prove Himself, He decided to test His disciples' faith by asking Phillip where to buy food and telling all of the disciples to feed the massive crowd. Although the disciples witnessed Jesus perform numerous miracles, including healing the sick and turning water into wine prior to this occasion, they could not fathom how He would feed a large crowd with 200 denarii worth of bread.

Two hundred denarii would be approximately $30-$35 today. Could you imagine being able to buy enough food to feed thousands of people with this amount of money? Naturally, this was not nearly enough food to feed more than 5,000 people. However, Jesus instructed His disciples to "have them sit down in groups of about fifty each." (v.10; Luke 9:14, NIV). Then, He took the food and gave thanks.

Notice the multitude of people could have looked at each other and began to leave or fight over the food. Instead, they sat and watched Jesus give thanks. As a result, they had more than enough to eat with leftovers included. As a result of the miracle, they realized who Jesus was. That was His purpose all along—to prove Himself by meeting their spiritual and physical needs. As a result of Jesus feeding more than 5,000 people with the lunch of a generous little boy, a massive multitude of people saw that He could create abundance out of limited resources.

Like he did with the little boy's lunch, God will multiply whatever you give Him. Friend, you must obey, trust God, and be thankful. These are actions that will result in Him blessing your vision. Not only will God provide what you need, He will provide more than enough. You will have resources leftover to share with others to support their visions.

If you need clarity regarding your vision, ask God to reveal His will for your life and to guide you. Ask Him to help you outline your goals and establish an action plan. Then, trust Him to help you do it. Based on spiritual guidance through (prayer, reading the word, and discernment), create a vision plan.

Wholehearted Faith

Partial faith in God equates to distrust in Him, but wholehearted faith involves faithfulness and trusting in God even when you do not know the outcome. When you possess wholehearted faith, you know that He will come through, for He is faithful to fulfill His promises and lead you to victory. Never doubt God's faithfulness!

There is a song by Elevation Worship entitled, "I Will Look Up" that says "I will look back and see that you are faithful. I look ahead believing you are able...." How encouraging it is to recount the faithfulness of God when you look back in retrospect! Hasn't He always proven Himself faithful? Why would He stop now? Why would you doubt Him, knowing that He is the same yesterday, today, and forevermore (Hebrews 13:8)? God is consistent, even when your faith wavers (2 Timothy 2:13). Know that He is faithful to fulfill His promises and watch them come to pass. He did not bring you here to leave you.

Faith is a journey. You may not always understand the twists and turns you encounter, but Jesus promises that His yoke is easy, and His burden is light (Matthew 11:30). So, be assured that God is with and will sustain you on your journey until He has accomplished all His promises in and through you. Paul the Apostle was "confident of this very thing, that he who began a good work in you will perfect it." (Philippians 1:6, NASB, 1977). God has not brought you this far to fail, but to prevail and finish well. You must have faith to obtain His promises.

The word builds and fuels faith. "Faith comes by hearing, and hearing by the word of God." (Romans 10:17, NKJV). Just as a seed needs water to grow daily, your spirit needs the Word of God to grow daily. The more you hear God's Word, the more insight you will receive, and the more insight you receive, the more you will believe Him. To increase your faith, think about and focus on the truth of Scripture, remember God's faithfulness to you in the past, and notice what He's doing in your present situation. When your mind is renewed, your faith will be fueled.

A person of mature faith knows that one's calling is best fulfilled when (s)he seeks and obeys the Lord despite challenges. (S)he also knows that no matter the circumstance, God is always present and faithful and works all things together for those who love Him, trust Him, and align with His will.

Do not be discouraged if you only have a small amount of faith. With it, you can still move mountains (Matthew 17:20). Use the measure of faith you have, and over time, it will increase. Jesus referred to the disciples, who were afraid during a violent storm, as men of little faith (see Matthew 8:26). On a separate occasion, the disciples were unable to cast a demon out of a boy at his father's request. So, the father asked Jesus to do so, while admitting, "Lord, I believe, help my unbelief!" (Mark 9:24, ESV).

Both the disciples and the boy's father had faith as demonstrated by their actions. The disciples attempted to cast out the unclean spirit after the boy's father asked them to, although they were unsuccessful at that moment. However, the father's faith still resulted in his son's healing, and the disciples' faith increased over time. Those disciples went on to preach the gospel amidst persecution, even until they were murdered for it, which is evidence of their mature faith development.

CHAPTER 7

Faith In Action (Part 2): Fight Fear with Faith

Faith is to believe what you do not see; the reward of this faith is to see what you believe.

Saint Augustine

We have learned that actions reflect beliefs and demonstrate faith. But in this chapter, I want to focus specifically on how faith operates and overpowers fear.

Seeing Jesus walking on the water, Peter the Apostle said to Him, "Lord, if it's you, tell me to come to you on the water." (Matthew 14:28, NIV), to which Jesus obliged. As he looked at Jesus, Peter successfully walked on water, but "when he saw the wind, he was afraid" and began to sink (Matthew 14:30, NIV). In other words, when Peter was focused on Jesus, he successfully defied the odds and walked on water. However, when he took his eyes off Jesus and focused on the violent wind and raging sea, he no longer did what Jesus told him to do, which was look toward Him. This led to anxiety and doubt. It's easy to doubt God when you're focused on your circumstances, but when you look to Him and focus on His faithfulness, then you can accomplish anything you set out to do.

As troubles increase, so should your faith, not fear. Peter became fearful and began to sink after he took his eyes off of Jesus and focused on the wind. He allowed his circumstances to interfere with his faith. When a problem or frustrations arise, focus on God and how He might be at work rather than focusing on the problem. When you have faith and focus on what God is doing, you will win in every area of life. Suddenly, the impossible will become possible, but you must keep your eyes on Christ, not your circumstances.

How can you have faith in God if your circumstances seem impossible? Let's look at how Joshua and Caleb responded when encountering a seemingly impossible circumstance (see Numbers 13-14). God instructed Moses while he was in the Desert of Paran to send 12 spies—one from each Israelite tribe to survey Canaan—the land of promise. The spies were instructed to observe the physical conditions of the land (e.g. its security, the capability of its soil to produce fruit, its vegetation, etc.) and to return with fruit grown in Canaan if possible. Upon their return, the spies brought back various fruits, and 10 spies discouraged the community of Israel from entering Canaan because giants were there. However, Joshua and Caleb encouraged the community to go in and seize the land.

Faith enables you to recognize God's ability despite your natural inability or challenges. When the 10 spies saw the sons of Anek who were big, tall people with incredibly long necks, they became timid. However, Joshua and Caleb saw those same giants, but were convinced that the Israelites could possess the land God promised to them. The 10 spies reported, "We felt as small as grasshoppers, and that's how we must have looked to them." (Numbers 13:33, GW). They looked at the sons of Anek compared to themselves and became intimidated and concluded they were not able to possess the land. While the 10 spies measured the giants against themselves and thought they looked like grasshoppers, Joshua and Caleb measured the giants against God and concluded that the giants looked like grasshoppers.

Do not measure your problem against yourself. Instead, measure your problem against your God. Is anything too hard for Him (Jeremiah 32:27)? Joshua and Caleb had faith despite facing the giants because they knew what God promised. They also knew that faith changes natural circumstances. So, no matter who occupied Canaan, Joshua and Caleb knew that God would give Israel the victory to inhabit the land He promised to them.

The enemy uses adversity to combat your confidence and tempt you to shrink back from pursuing your purpose, but God uses it to strengthen you to persevere. Do not limit yourself to what you see in the natural realm. Doing so could cause your confidence to quiver. You may be facing a seemingly impossible situation, but know that "with God, all things are possible." (Matthew 19:26, NIV). Embrace faith instead of fear.

Fear does not come from God, for He "did not give us a spirit that makes us afraid but a spirit of power and love and self-control." (2 Timothy 1:7, NCV). Fear is a tactic the enemy uses in his attempts to inhibit you from pursuing your purpose and attaining God's best for you. Moreover, John, the beloved disciple, expressed, "perfect love expels all fear." (1 John 4:18, NASB). When you understand that God loves you perfectly and only wants the best for you, like Joshua and Caleb, you know that the Lord wants to do exceptional things in your life. You choose to meditate on God's promises and magnify Him rather than your circumstances as you pursue purpose. Realizing that you have nothing to fear, you refuse to allow fear to reign. You choose faith over fear.

As a result of the negative reports of the 10 spies and the fear of Israel that followed it, that generation, except Caleb, Joshua, and those 20 years of age and younger died before God permitted the

Israelites to enter Canaan. They spent 40 years wandering in the wilderness before entering the Promised Land. Refuse to allow fear to influence your decisions. Refuse to allow fear to prevent you from experiencing what God promised you.

Scripture says "we walk by faith, not by sight." (2 Corinthians 5:7, ESV). Walking by faith involves trusting our Father despite being unaware of when or how He will create a solution. Ponder the words of King Solomon:

> "As you do not know the path of the wind, or how the body is formed in a mother's womb, so you cannot understand the work of God, the Maker of all things."
>
> Ecclesiastes 11:5 (NIV)

You will always encounter challenging circumstances, but do not become fixated on what you see with your natural eyes. Instead, use your spiritual insight. Naturally, you cannot see how a baby is developing in the womb every second of his or her development. Despite modern technology, there are things that cannot be observed. So it is with the things of the spirit. God is working and manifesting things behind the scenes that you cannot perceive. So do not be fixated on negative reports. Whose report will you believe (Isaiah 53:1)? Refuse to be dismayed by what you can see, but be excited by what you can't see! Fix your eyes on the Father, and trust that He is doing exceedingly, abundantly, above all you could ask, think, or imagine (Ephesians 3:20).

Walking by faith requires total trust in God, not in one's own energy, ability, or expertise. Author J.P. Moreland writes in *Love Your God with All Your Mind: The Role of Reason in the Life of the Soul,* "Faith is a power or skill to act in accordance with the nature of the kingdom of God, a trust in what we have reason to believe is true." It is resolving to believe that He is who He says He is. It is confidence in the character and revelation of who God is. It is trusting that He is faithful to provide victory no matter the challenges you experience. As Tania Runyan explains in *By Rote: Windows to the Soul*, "Faith, of course, is not about *feeling* that everything will be okay, but *knowing* it." When you have faith, you know that God holds the future in His hands. Therefore, He has already taken care of the details pertaining to your future. You just have to live by faith, trusting that He is working on your behalf.

Faith sees the end from the beginning. It is not based on favorable circumstances, but on the character of God. When you have faith, you have a disposition of expectancy. This is not passive. Faith is active. Faith influences your footsteps. The Bible says, "Fight the good fight of the faith..."(1 Timothy 6:12, NIV). Faith is what led David to fight Goliath (see 1 Samuel 17). David was confident that He would defeat Goliath because he represented the God of Israel (1 Samuel 17:45).

From David's victory, we see that "man's extremity is God's opportunity." (Flavel, n.d.). Years before David—the overlooked youngest son—went to check on his brothers during battle, God was preparing him to defeat Goliath. David was a shepherd boy who fought wild animals to protect his sheep. God used David's skills and confidence as he fought Goliath. When David approached Goliath, he did not have any armor for battle, but he had all he needed to defeat his enemy. To onlookers, David seemed to be no match for the Philistine giant, but David knew that he had been empowered by God to defeat the enemy.

Like David, when you have faith, you will embrace every challenge, knowing that the battle is not yours; it's the Lord's (2 Chronicles 20:15). Be like David. Don't focus on the natural circumstances and odds stacked against you. Instead, look with eyes of faith. See your victorious outcome from the beginning. Get excited!

Faith is what moves the heart of God. In her sermon entitled *Fine Tune Your Hearing (Part 3)*, Christine Caine says, "Faith is the currency of heaven. When we pray by faith, we move God, and when God's moved, He moves mountains, and He destroys giants in our lives." Faith is confidence in God's promises. Faith is always present tense. It is now. You may believe in God for something you expect to manifest in the future, but to have faith, you must believe it now because faith is a current possession.

Don't limit what God can do in your life by dwelling on what you see in the natural realm. You serve a supernatural God who has unlimited opportunities and resources in store for you. Just because you might not see a way doesn't mean that God doesn't have a way. Take the limits off and live with anticipation!

Operate in faith, not fear. After the 10 spies discouraged the Israelites with the negative report, Joshua and Caleb provided a positive report (see Numbers 14). They knew they were well able and that the only thing that could hinder them was lack of faith. Joshua and Caleb knew that the majority is not always correct. It does not matter how big the task may appear. When you measure the enemy by God, the enemy is dwarfed. The prophet Isaiah asked, "Who has believed our report?" (Isaiah 53:1, NKJV). Be like Joshua and Caleb and believe the Lord's report. Fight fear with faith!

Refuse To Worry

Anxiety or distress is uneasiness of mind caused by fear or misfortune. Anxiety often occurs when hardship arises, but God wants adversity to strengthen your faith in Him. He desires that you trust and cling to Him when challenges occur, and He desires to develop within you the dynamic faith that the great witnesses in the Hall of Faith had (see Hebrews 11). So, do not allow anxiety to cloud your vision nor discourage you to doubt God's promises.

Matthew 6:31 (KJV) says, "Therefore take no thought, saying..." A thought unspoken is alive. It can live or die. As one thinks, so is (s)he (Proverbs 23:7). The great philosopher Lao Tzu once said, "Watch your thoughts, they become your words; watch your words, they become your actions; watch your actions, they become your habits; watch your habits, they become your character; watch your character, it becomes your destiny." Whatever you think about, you magnify. If you dwell on anxious thoughts, they will become words which will form habits and eventually lead to a doubt-filled destiny.

Jesus instructs us not to be anxious about tomorrow (Matthew 6:34). Abraham Lincoln said, "The best thing about the future is that it comes one day at a time." It is important to live one day at a time worry-free while focusing on the present. So, do not worry about the outcome of your circumstances. That would only lead to frustration.

Just because you have not identified a solution does not mean there is not one. In Philippians 4:6 (NKJV), we are told to "Be careful for nothing; but in every thing by prayer and supplication with thanksgiving let our requests be made known unto God." In other words, do not be anxious. Pray regarding every situation you encounter and allow the Holy Spirit's promptings to guide your decisions. Make it a habit to pray continually (1 Thessalonians 5:17) and "fix your thoughts on what is true, and honorable, and right, and pure, and lovely, and admirable..." (Philippians 4:8, NLT). Choose not to waste today by worrying about the future. Instead, pray and proceed as the Lord leads.

CHAPTER 8

Change Your Words, Change Your World

The tongue has the power of life and death, and those who love it will eat its fruit.

Proverbs 18:21

Do you know that your words have power to direct you toward God's plan for your life? Jeremiah 29:11 says God has a plan and a future for you, but sometimes your challenges may cause you to question this. However, God wants you to gradually see and pursue the future that He has for you. How do you get there? Where do you start? With declaration.

Words are the most powerful things that exist—they govern everything because, as Pastor Kenneth Copeland rightly said, "this is a word-created, word-dominated, word-upheld universe." In the beginning, when God saw that the earth was empty and dark, He *said*, "Let there be light," and there was light (Genesis 1:1-3, KJV). With His words, God "calls things into existence that do not exist." (Romans 4:17, CSB). Notice that God did not think things into motion. He verbally declared creation into manifestation. In Matthew 21:18-22, the disciples witnessed the power of (Jesus') spoken words firsthand. In like manner, when you declare things aloud, you prophesy what will occur. This is why Jesus said to His disciples, "if anyone says to this mountain, 'Go, throw yourself into the sea,' and does not doubt in their heart but believes that what they say will happen, it will be done for them." (see Mark 11:23, NIV).

The Power of The Tongue

With your tongue, you have the power to set the course for your life. In James 3, the tongue is compared to a small rudder that controls a ship (James 3:4). If you see a ship rudder, you will notice that it is very small compared to the rest of the ship. However, the rudder is what the captain uses to steer the ship in the direction (s)he wants it to go. Even if a huge storm approaches the ship, the rudder still directs the ship accordingly. Like that rudder, your tongue can be used to steer your life in the direction you want it to go.

Use your tongue to direct your future. Agree with God and align your thoughts and words with His. Speak life, knowing that what God promised, He will perform. Keep declaring that He who called you and made promises to you is faithful (1 Thessalonians 5:24). Declare that He is perfecting what concerns you (Psalms 138:8). Declare that He will complete everything He started in your life (Philippians 1:6). When you declare God's faithfulness, you move in the right direction—toward the future He designed for you.

Even amidst the storms of life, you can use your words to change your circumstances. Do not allow your present to dictate your future. In other words, do not say what you see by focusing on your circumstances. Instead, say what you want to see in order to change your circumstances. In his song "No Limits", the psalmist Israel Houghton challenges, "Say what you heard so you can see what you said." Here, he is referring to declaring God's promises so that they will manifest. When you declare God's promises, you will experience them.

What Are You Declaring?

When He commissioned Joshua to lead the Israelites to the Promised Land, God said, "this book of the law shall not depart from your mouth." (Joshua 1:8, ESV). The law referred to God's word. In other words, for Joshua to succeed, he needed to declare the word at all times. Why? Because as Pastor EB Herman says, "if you want to see something manifested in your life, you release your faith through your words."

Where should your words come from? Scripture. "All scripture is God-breathed....so that the servant of God may be thoroughly equipped for every good work." (2 Timothy 3:16-17, NIV). When you declare scripture, you align with the good works God equipped you to do (Ephesians 2:10). Being tempted by Satan in the wilderness, Jesus firmly protested, "Man shall not live by bread alone, but by every word that comes forth from the mouth of God." (Matthew 4:4, ESV). It was the word of God that sustained Jesus and empowered Him to withstand temptation in the wilderness. It was the word that caused Satan to flee.

What you hear, you will say and begin to believe. "So then faith *comes* by hearing, and hearing by the word of God.", Paul, the apostle, wrote (Romans 10:17, NKJV). If you listen to someone or something long enough, you will repeat the information. What are you listening to? Are you listening to what God is saying to you? If so, you will declare it. And what you say, you will see. When you declare God's word, His word will form pictures on the canvas of your mind, and that's what you will move toward. Declaring God's word will lead to fulfilling the plan He has for you (Jeremiah 29:11).

How do you get God to move? By confessing His word instead of your circumstances. How do you get God to answer your prayers? By speaking from His viewpoint instead of yours. How do you begin to see your vision manifest? Speak God's word over it. As you speak God's promises over your dreams, you'll see them begin to take shape. I dare you to speak God's word over your situation and watch Him manifest His promises!

Write your vision and make it plain. Then, begin to declare those things. You may not know everything about God's purpose for your life, for you know in part and see in part (1 Corinthians 13:9), but begin to make positive declarations. *"I'm going to do something amazing! I'm going to impact lives for the better. My children and future generations will succeed. I'm setting a new course for my family and communities."* Even when obstacles arise, you have to declare, *"If God is for me, who can be against me?"* (Romans 8:31).

Friend, what are you thinking and declaring today? What are you declaring over your life? What do you want to see happen? Understand that your words have tremendous power. Remember that you have the power to direct your future. This does not depend upon your current circumstances. Instead, this can and will change your circumstances, and if necessary, the direction of your life, to help you fulfill your vision. So, speak to your situation as if it could change tomorrow because it could!

Verbalize Your Vision

Picture words as seeds and (verbally) declaring them as seed planting. Your words are seeds that take root through declarations, and you reap their harvest. The Bible says, "Death and life are in the power of the tongue: and they that love it shall eat the fruit thereof." (Proverbs 18:21, KJV). That's why it's important to speak your vision into existence (Romans 4:17). When you declare your vision aloud by stating what you want to happen or by praising God in advance for accomplishing it, you are sowing what you speak, and you will reap a harvest of the fruit of your words in return.

When I was in college, I wanted to study abroad. Long before I ever looked into study abroad programs, I'd speak the opportunity into existence. I'd pray, "*Lord, thank you for my study abroad opportunity. Thank you for my passport (which I did not possess at the time). Thank you for the scholarship (which I didn't have at the time).*" I'd constantly thank God for opportunities and resources to study abroad before creating a plan to study internationally. As time passed, I came across opportunities to learn about study abroad programs and scholarships. Before I knew it, I was studying in Seville, Spain during summer 2011. It all started with speaking it into existence!

Watch what you are saying because your mouth can be a destructive force or an instrument of blessing that impacts your life and those around you. Do not give life to negative thoughts by speaking them out. Instead, declare that your dreams and visions will manifest. Speak over them and declare that you will conquer your challenges, for you can do all things through Christ who strengthens you (Romans 8:37; Philippians 4:13). Choose to agree with God's word, and release words of faith. Believe and declare what He says about you. You are blessed and not cursed. You are healed and not sick. You are whole and not broken. You are free and not bound. Let this sink in. Don't be afraid to declare who you are.

Understand that every word you speak matters. Blessings proceed out of our mouths and work immediately, whether we see the manifestation or not. Therefore, speak life to your future. As you make positive declarations, God will create opportunities that will align with them. When you speak His word over your vision, your talk will affect your walk, and your walk will affect your work. No matter what you may be facing today, let the words of your mouth lead you in the way you desire. Declare aloud because your words count and matter!

Your words have lasting impact. Although they may seem insignificant to you, your words are life changing! While in undergrad, I often praised God for the opportunity to attend graduate school. Years before I ever applied to graduate school, I prayed, "*Lord, I thank you for the opportunity to attend grad school on a full ride. I have no idea where I will apply or where I will go, but I thank you that my master's degree will be paid in full.*" While praying and thanking God in advance, I researched different graduate programs and I participated in undergraduate summer research programs to prepare for grad school.

In 2012, I received two offers to attend graduate school on full scholarships. One was the opportunity to earn a master's, with the possibility of extended funding to earn a doctorate degree depending upon my academic performance. The other offer included funding to earn a doctorate degree. I accepted the latter. It all started with declaring in advance, "*Lord, I thank you for the opportunity to attend graduate school without having to pay for it. Thank you for my advanced degrees. Thank you for your provision.*" Friend, I could not afford to pay for international study nor graduate school out of pocket but, I knew the power of speaking those opportunities into existence. I knew that against all odds, one touch of God's favor could take me from *no* funding for grad school to having more than enough!

During my time in grad school, I journaled often. After each entry, I signed off "*Lois Harmon, Ph.D" or Dr. Lois Harmon, Ph.D*". This was long before I advanced to candidacy, but I knew the power of not only verbally declaring what I wanted to accomplish, but also seeing written declarations of it. The more I journaled and signed off on each entry, the closer I became to making my title a reality. As you can see, even when opportunities and accomplishments are intangible, you can make declarations, and eventually you will see what you say. Your declarations determine your destiny. So, say what you want to see. Speak life!

CHAPTER 9

Trust God (Part 1): Divine Time

Faith and trust are so connected that we cannot separate them.

Joyce Meyer

One of the greatest abilities God has given each one of us is our ability to trust Him. Trust is simply confidence in the reliability, truth, ability, or strength of someone or something (Oxford University Press, 2022b).

There is no evidence of trust without a test. Let's look at Abram [(later named Abraham) see Genesis 17]. This was a man who grew up in a pagan family but heard the voice of God telling him to leave his homeland and travel to an unknown place. Some time later, God told Abraham to sacrifice Isaac—his son (Genesis 22:2), which he was willing to do until God told him not to (see Genesis 22:12). The Bible says, "He considered that God is able to raise *people* even from the dead...." (Hebrews 11:19, NASB), and *"...Abraham believed God, and it was credited to him as righteousness..."* (James

2:23, NASB). Not only did Abraham prepare to offer his son as a sacrifice to God, he also left his family and all familiar territory (Genesis 12:4-5) because He trusted God.

There is incredible power in trusting the Lord. Abraham had unwavering trust in God, which resulted in rewards that far supersede his time spent on earth, for they still occur today (see Genesis 12:2; 15:5; 17:5-6). Because He trusted God, he has an ongoing legacy as evident in every nation on the earth (see Genesis 17:16, 19-20; Galatians 3:29).

Will you, like Abraham, trust God against all odds? Since He has called you to fulfill His will, you can trust Him to accomplish it through you. If you wholeheartedly trust God, you will fulfill your purpose.

Divine Time

When trials arise and your vision is not being fulfilled according to your timetable, it can be difficult to fully believe and firmly stand on the truth of God's promises. Yet it is important to know that the Lord is trustworthy, for everything He promises He will perform (Romans 4:21). There is an appointed time set by God to fulfill the desires of your heart. His time is the best time, and the desires that He will fulfill are those He has given you according to His will.

God does not always provide a timeframe for performing His promises. You may not always know nor understand God's timing, but know that just because things aren't happening on your timetable doesn't mean they aren't going to happen. God works on His timetable, not ours. What we consider to be a long time could be a short time from His perspective. To God, who sees things in light of eternity, a day is as a thousand years (2 Peter 3:8). Seeing the end from the beginning, the Lord is not slow to fulfill His promise as some count slowness (2 Peter 3:9). Although God may be moving slowly from our perspective, He is always right on time because His timing is perfect.

Are you believing God for something that has yet to manifest? It's easy to become discouraged when things don't happen according to your timetable, but do not let the clock or calendar discourage you. During my first year of graduate school, I designed a research proposal for my master's thesis, and I was approved by my committee to move forward with the data collection. Shortly after receiving permission from my committee to move forward with my research project, I was notified by a stakeholder at the prospective research site that I would not be granted permission to collect data there.

Prior to being disallowed to collect data for my research project, I was so excited about the research design I created! I made contacts and invested time at a local school (the proposed research site) to set a foundation for my research project, but unfortunately, it was not enough to move forward with conducting my research. When I was notified that I was not welcome to collect more data for the research project at the school, I was so disappointed. I even cried as a result of feeling so deflated. After reading the rejection email, I just allowed tears to flow. It was from the principal of a local school in an area I was new to. Although I had her permission, I had not quite built trust with all of the stakeholders involved due to my being new to the area and not having many relationships within the school and local community.

Not too long after I was notified of not being allowed to conduct research at the school to analyze and observe teachers' literacy practices, I met with my advisors to discuss an alternate plan. One of my advisors recommended studying pre-service teachers (instead of in-service teachers). I had no idea at the time that I shifted my focus from in-service teachers' practices to pre-service teacher preparation that this would set the foundation for my career path in teacher education moving forward. God can truly take disappointment and shift you toward something more fulfilling.

Before attending graduate school, my plan was to move back to Florida after completing my studies. However, during my last year of graduate school, I decided to apply for a prestigious post-doc position in California. Although I knew that I would not be passionate about this position, I felt that I should pursue it to obtain more research experience (since remaining in the academy and continuing the research pipeline were widely-held expectations for anyone obtaining a PhD from a research-intensive institution). However, God had other plans for me. While waiting to hear back about the post-doc, I decided to remain in CA (rather than move back to Fl, only to have to move back to CA if I was awarded the fellowship). I also decided to apply for other jobs in CA while awaiting the decision. During my time of waiting for notification about the post-doc, my current job position became vacant. I made the final round of applicants for the post-doc, but was not awarded the fellowship.

As I look in retrospect, I realize that my remaining in California was never for me to pursue the post-doc, but for me to do what I am currently doing. I did not understand why I was not awarded the post-doc until I received a tenure-track faculty position shortly thereafter. God had my best interest at heart all along.

Thankfully, God did not allow me to fully pursue something that would turn out to be unfulfilling for me. I am so glad He knows me better than I know myself. The Apostle Paul puts it this way: "....all things work together for the good of those who love God, who are called according to His purpose." (Romans 8:28, CSB). By default, God always has His purpose in mind for every area of our lives. Consider this scripture:

> The mind of a person plans his way, But the Lord directs his steps.
>
> Proverbs 16:9 (NASB)

It never ceases to amaze me that God is always working behind the scenes to orchestrate His will for us even when we are unaware. So, submit to His timing and trust Him. Do not allow the waiting to discourage you from being hopeful in His promises to give you your heart's desires. Instead, begin to thank God for what He has planned for you. Scripture says that those who hope in the Lord will never be put to shame (Psalms 25:3) or disappointed (Isaiah 49:23). After walking with God for more than half of my life, I can attest that He is faithful. Although everything did not occur the way I expected, I now understand that God always allowed what was best for me.

Trust God's timing. Timing is essential for everything. The scriptures promise us that God has an appointed time for all things (Habakkuk 2:3). You may not know the appointed time, but, like Solomon, you are invited to believe that "there is a time for everything, and a season for every activity under the heavens." (Ecclesiastes 3:1, NIV). No matter how long you've been waiting, no matter how impossible it may seem, have faith and know your appointed time is coming.

Responding to Disappointments

Choosing to wait on God is not an immunity to disappointment. Disappointment is an emotional response to a failed expectation, hope, or desire. It may be tempting to become disappointed when our plans don't unfold the way we envisioned. We will experience disappointment with things and people from time to time. Maybe you're in a difficult season right now. Maybe you did not get the job you wanted, or the promotion you desired, or the medical report you expected. Whatever the circumstance, the truth is: disappointment is inevitable.

While disappointment is inevitable, discouragement is not. Discouragement is a feeling of despair or despondency. This may occur as a result of an unexpected setback or difficulty, but discouragement is also a choice. Take a look at 1 Samuel 30:6. "David was greatly distressed because the men were talking of stoning him; each one was bitter in spirit because of his sons and daughters. But David found strength in the Lord his God." (NIV). Facing a devastating defeat as a result of his city being destroyed, families taken captive, and his men plotting to stone him, David chose to encourage himself. Despite his men plotting to kill him, David did not sit still and think *"I'm going to die soon. So, I should start making a will"*. No, he encouraged himself. He said, "I will bless the Lord at all times; His praise shall continually be in my mouth." (Psalms 34:1, ESV). David chose to praise God instead of being discouraged.

The disappointment of being told I could not collect data for my master's project became a decisive moment. Although I was very sad, disappointed, and discouraged, I became more resilient. Instead of staying stuck, I shifted my focus and kept my momentum. This shift fueled a passion within me that became my new research focus —teacher preparation for supporting the literacy development of elementary students, especially English learners.

If you are discouraged, you do not have to remain in that state. Instead, find a reason to rejoice, and move forward. Recount the Father's faithfulness and focus on the opportunities before you. As you reflect on the Father's faithfulness despite the disappointment, remember the encouraging words of Apostle Paul, "forgetting those things which are behind and reaching forward to those things which are ahead...press toward the goal for the prize of the upward call of God in Christ Jesus." (Philippians 3:13-14, NKJV). Be encouraged today my friend as you pursue the dreams God placed in your heart, and know that He will bring them to pass.

Navigating the job market included some disappointments. I initially wanted a full-time, tenure-track teaching position at a community college or university in Dallas, TX, or CA. While looking into jobs, I only saw openings for adjunct positions and other jobs I was not interested in. I initially thought "*If only I received the post-doc...*" However, during the season of searching for jobs, God directed me to be wise and strategic in my search in a way that expanded my network. I often meditated on "*...seek first His kingdom and His righteousness, and all these things will be given to you as well.*" (Matthew 6:33, NIV) and "*Be still and know that I am God...*" (Psalms 46:10, BSB). Although I did not know where I would end up or what I would be doing, I sought and trusted God. As a result, I took a job at a university I had never heard of in a city I had never heard of (similar to my graduate school choice). I also interviewed for and accepted a job I was not initially interested in. I'm still in awe that I love doing a job that I initially assumed I would not like when I saw the job description.

Within my job, all of my research skills and knowledge from previous work experiences (leadership, organizational understanding, and teacher education) are being applied. God is also strengthening, stirring, and extending my administrative and managerial skills as well as my creativity. It's an amazing experience!

While encouraging and exhorting the Philippians, the Apostle Paul advised them to imitate him as he refuses to look back and strains to move forward (see 3:13, NIV) to pursue purpose. He was not content to wallow around in every difficulty he encountered. Instead, he trusted the Lord, knowing that He always has the final say. Paul knew that difficulty would not prevent him from reaching destiny. He knew that God would perform His promises. He believed because he knew that setbacks are temporary, but God's promises are permanent. Paul knew that God's Word would not return void (Isaiah 55:11). Like Paul, I kept hoping and believing. Although I did not see a way, I knew that God would make a way.

Be encouraged today knowing that God finishes what He starts. You just have to believe. Believe that He will right every wrong on your behalf. Believe His favor is greater than your fear. Be encouraged knowing that He is at work completing what He started in you (Philippians 1:6). You have the advantage because you have His favor upon your life (Psalm 90:17).

You may have experienced a setback and felt disappointed, but no matter what happened, God has a new opportunity in store, for He makes all things new (Revelation 21:5, AMPC). Know that God is aware of every disappointment, and the good news is He can use every difficulty you experience to further His purpose for your life. Even when things don't go the way you planned, trust that the Creator of the universe has His hand on you. He didn't bring you this far to leave you now, for He knows where you are (Job 23:10) and He is leading you (Psalms 32:8). He is turning your setbacks into comebacks.

God is not a God of defeat. So, disappointment is not the finale. Do not allow your current situation to discourage you from believing in your dreams. Do not allow the magnitude of your dreams to discourage you from pursuing your purpose. As the Brazilian lyricist and novelist Paulo Coelho said, "Remember your dreams and fight for them. You must know what you want from life. There is just one thing that makes your dream become impossible: the fear of failure." Right now, release your disappointments to the heavenly Father. Submit your situation to Him and rest assured that He has a triumphant finish for you. You won't be disappointed for long.

God can use what disappointed you to work in your favor. His plan can override any setback. Know that for every setback, God has a comeback. For every conflict, He has a resolution. For every disillusionment, He has gratification. Trust that God is orchestrating the best opportunities for you. Trust Him with your future. Choose to rejoice always (Philippians 4:7) and trust the Lord to do great things. You may experience temporary disappointment, but know that God is working behind the scenes on your behalf to arrange things for your good. Make a decision to bless the Lord at all times and thank Him for His plan to give you a strong finish!

CHAPTER 10

Trust God (Part 2): Waiting Patiently

Trust in the Lord with all your heart; and lean not to your own understanding. In all your ways acknowledge Him, and He shall direct your path.

Proverbs 3:5-6 (AKJV)

A microwave warms meals in minutes, amazon delivers products within 24-48 hours, and streaming platforms make television shows and movies immediately accessible. The internet, smart phones, and social media provide instant access to information, and Instacart prevents us from waiting in lines. What do all of these have in common? They are all convenient and cater to our impatience. So, we are often conditioned to not wait. Why are we so impatient? Because we want what we want immediately.

No matter the technological advancements and resources at our disposal that provide convenience, some things require patience. Sharpening your skills takes time. Building your business requires patience. Career attainment requires patience. Pursuing purpose demands patience, and the ability to endure even in the midst of difficulty. In the New Testament, the author of Hebrews advises, "let us run with perseverance the race marked out for us, fixing our eyes on Jesus, the Pioneer and Perfecter of faith." (Hebrews 1:1-2, NIV).

Patience, as Pastor Charles Stanley describes, is "the quiet, uncomplaining endurance under stress or annoyance. It is the will to wait."(Stanley, 2021a). Patience is a gift from God through the Holy Spirit. It is a virtue that God develops within us to act according to His will. Patience is the grace to wait. Waiting on God demonstrates trust in Him. It is critical for experiencing God's best, and it impacts all of our endeavors. When we wait on God, we act according to His timing, which is what pursuing purpose is all about—-doing what He calls us to do when He calls us to do it.

Patience is a Virtue

Scripture frequently instructs us to wait on God as it outlines the advantages of this as well as the consequences for forsaking to do so (see Psalm 37:9; Isaiah 40:31; James 1:12; Hebrews 10:36; Proverbs 14:29). Psalms 27:14 (NASB) presents a command we must follow: "Wait for the Lord; Be strong and let your heart take courage; Yes, wait for the Lord." Notice "wait" is mentioned twice and courage is also mentioned. King David knew that waiting on God may feel uncomfortable or seem impossible because patience is one of the most challenging disciplines to practice. Waiting patiently while pursuing purpose is an active demonstration of trust in God. Rather than being passive, this involves actively listening, being still, and only acting according to the omniscient Father's guidance.

Patiently pursuing purpose will require being pushed to your limits and overcoming obstacles. When encountering unpleasant circumstances that are challenging to navigate, most of us want to bypass those experiences. We want instant relief and immediate answers. We want to control our circumstances and create desired results instead of waiting on God for guidance. Therefore, strength is needed to endure patiently. The prophet Isaiah reminds us that when we wait upon the Lord, we will gain new strength (Isaiah 40:31) as He acts on our behalf (Isaiah 64:4). On the contrary, impatience is always costly and often leads to trouble and distress. This is commonly apparent in the forms of unnecessary debt, frustration, and other negative consequences that result from immediate gratification or the lack of patience. It is wise to always wait upon God because He knows what we need, and He always has the best in store for us.

Patience is essential for pursuing purpose, for this pursuit cannot be expedited. Paul told the Hebrews to "imitate those who through faith and patience inherit the promises." (Hebrews 6:12, NKJV). After Abraham patiently waited, God's promise was fulfilled (Hebrews 6:15). Unlike the Israelites who were near the Promised Land when they talked themselves out of it, Caleb knew they could defeat the giants in Canaan (see Numbers 13:26-33). Speaking to Moses, he boldly declared "Let's go at once to take the land. We can certainly conquer it!" (Numbers 13:30, NLT). Although Caleb had faith, he had to patiently wait for 40 years to enter the Promised land as a result of other Israelites' doubt. Through it all, He experienced what God promised him (see Joshua 14:6-15).

Learning to wait upon the Lord is essential for fulfilling purpose. He always has a reason for instructing us to wait. After countless valuable lessons on patience, I have learned to wait on God because that is the only way I will be satisfied. I believe He is worthy of my patience and has the perfect timing. God does not always fulfill our desires or do so when we want Him to or in the ways we expect Him to, but He always does so according to His will and timing, and He is never late.

Waiting upon the Lord is a decision at our disposal. Though he had many opportunities to defeat King Saul in order to become the King of Israel, David decided to wait upon God and trust His timing to be appointed king (see 1 Samuel 24:10-11; 26:10-11). David understood that submitting to the Father's will requires patience. His patience resulted in God appointing him king of His chosen nation (2 Samuel 5:3) and a forefather of His beloved Son (Matthew 1:1).

If you patiently pursue your purpose, you will fulfill it. Remember, God is true to His word. So, if He said it, He will manifest it. God promises to meet all of our needs (Philippians 4:19). Take Him up on His offer. Stand firm, knowing that He will fulfill His promises. They will not return void. Live out God's promises no matter the circumstances nor what people say. Do not lose sight of God's promises.

Are you willing to wait and only do what God tells you to do according to His timing? Know that you can never go wrong by listening to Him. Allow the Lord to cultivate patience within you and rely on His divine viewpoint. Remember that He is for you (Psalms 56:9) as He desires the best for His children. As you wait patiently upon the Lord, He will direct you according to His divine timing.

Trust His Timing

While awaiting your appointed time, you must not throw away your confidence. "Though your vision tarry, wait for it." (Habakkuk 2:3, NASB). Remain steadfast and unmovable. Be like Jacob who wrestled with the angel until he received his blessing from the Lord (see Genesis 32:22–32; Hosea 12:4). Be like David who confidently fought and defeated Goliath. There is a song by Sanctus Real called "Confidence." The song says, "Give me faith like Daniel in the lion's den. Give me hope like Moses in the wilderness. Give me a heart like David. Lord be my defense so I can face my giants with confidence."

Friend, you must have confidence that our Father has an appointed time to fulfill the desires of your heart, and He has empowered you to do all that He called you to.

Our God is faithful. No matter how long you've been waiting, no matter how impossible it may seem, have faith and know your appointed time is coming. You must trust His timing because timing is everything. It is wise to confidently trust His plan instead of your own thinking (Proverbs 3:5). We know in part and see in part (1 Corinthians 13:12). It is not your job to figure everything out, but to trust Him wholeheartedly to perform His perfect plan. He can use things we expect, or He can do something totally unexpected. You must trust that God sees the big picture and knows what is best for you and the best timing to manifest His promises. It is awesome that we can always trust Him and the plans that He has for us. Most of all, it pleases God, and He desires to perform and accomplish His good, acceptable, and perfect plan. So, seek, trust, and wait on Him daily.

What are you believing God for? What are you anticipating? Refuse to allow your present circumstances to dictate your feelings. You might be tempted to believe that your dreams will never come to pass. You might be tempted to throw in the towel because things are not happening according to your timetable. Perhaps you received a daunting medical report. You may feel that you're at your wit's end and there is no way out. But, those are all lies! Refuse to believe the lies! Instead, declare the truth. His word is true, and He is faithful to watch over and perform it. It's your job to have faith. Know that He is *I am* (Exodus 3:14)—whatever you need Him to be in any situation. If you need a doctor, He'll heal you. If you need a lawyer, He'll fight for you. If you're in trouble, He'll rescue you and be your refuge. If you need direction, He is the ultimate compass who will guide you. God is always available and accessible for providing whatever you need.

It is for you to trust God no matter your circumstance. Do not only trust God for circumstances to change, but throughout circumstances that occur. As God assured the Israelites, when you trust Him, you will be established and successful (see 2 Chronicles 20:1-30). Dare to trust Him even if it does not make sense. Sometimes the only way you learn to do something is when you have no other option. You have to recognize: There is no alternative. You must resolve to trust God!

Patience and trust in God go hand-in-hand. When we truly trust God, we are able to patiently endure adversity and successfully pursue purpose, knowing that God is faithful to guide us effectively. How are you called to wait upon God right now? Will you use this as an opportunity to increase patience and trust in God?

CHAPTER 11

Divine Appointments: Share Your Vision

Write the vision; make it plain on tablets, so he may run who reads it.

Habakkuk 2:2 (ESV)

God not only made us for Himself, but He made us for each other. He made us to need one another. He made us to cooperate and to fellowship one with the other.

Charles Stanley

Before He created the world, God had a plan for your life including the people He would connect you with. God places people in our lives to help us reach our destinies. Those people may connect us with key figures to thrust us forward into our God-given purposes.

The summer before I began graduate school, I participated in a research scholars program which paired me with a faculty mentor who I will refer to as Hilary. After meeting me in person and learning about my research interests, Hilary introduced me to one of her colleagues who I will refer to as Ashley. Ironically, the faculty mentor (Hilary) who I was paired with did not mentor me, but the person she introduced me to (Ashley) became one of my key mentors throughout my graduate school experience. I was initially disappointed that I did not receive the mentoring I expected from the original faculty mentor I was paired with, but looking back in retrospect, I realized that God used her to connect me with who he really wanted to mentor me. I rarely saw or communicated with Ashley during the summer, but months later after I began grad school, I met with Ashley to discuss my research interests, and she became very instrumental in my research process and networking.

Divine appointments are orchestrated by God. You never know who God may use and how He may use them to incorporate you into their networks. When I initially met with Hilary, I never expected her to introduce me to anyone else, but she decided to based on my research interests. I realized later on that it was Ashley who God wanted to mentor me all along, but He had to use Hilary to make the connection and introduce us. So, both women were instrumental in my graduate school journey. Although Hilary did not mentor me, she was very helpful in my graduate school career and beyond. It was Hilary who let me borrow books that were very helpful for informing my qualifying exams and it was Hilary who was instrumental in helping me work and gain professional development in teacher education. She told me about a job as well as hired me for my first lecture position right out of grad school. So, God orders our steps in marvelous ways. We just have to trust Him. Pastor IV Hilliard (2015) often says, "God is raising up somebody somewhere to use their power, ability, and influence to help me.", and that is what God did when he assigned Hilary as my faculty mentor.

Remember, God can use anyone to help you. So, treat everyone you encounter with kindness and respect, not because you expect something in return, but because you exemplify Christ in doing so. This can also potentially result in a blessing in the form of a new relationship or connection. You never know who God will use in your life. So, never overlook nor condescend anyone.

Before we can fully appreciate the people God placed in our lives to help us pursue purpose, we have to understand why they are there. Purposes are founded upon counsel. Without counsel, purposes are confused, but in a multitude of counselors, safety is present, and purposes are understood and established (Proverbs 15:22). God never intended for you to walk alone, for He created people to be relational. That is why He placed you within your family, communities, and networks. In addition to providing help through the Comforter (John 14:26), God also provides people to walk side-by-side with you. These people may play different roles, including but not limited to: parents, siblings, other relatives, mentors, confidantes, coworkers, and co-laborers in your vision. For me, these people include: my parents, dear friends, former college advisors, and colleagues. These people are my safety network. God often uses them to share their discernment and best judgment to inform my decision-making.

In the second year of his reign, Nebuchadnezzar ordered for all of the wise men in his kingdom to be executed after realizing that no one could reveal his dream or its interpretation (see Daniel 2). However, Daniel sought the support of his godly friends, and together, they prayed for God to give Daniel the interpretation of the king's dream so their lives would be spared (Daniel 2:17-18). Unlike most of us, Daniel did not waste time worrying. Instead, he called on his prayer partners.

Do you, like Daniel, have a safety network? If not, you should create one by identifying at least two people you can rely on to pray with you. Choose believers who know the word and will pray in agreement with you. In Matthew 18:19-20 (ESV), Jesus plainly states, "if two of you agree on earth about anything they ask, it will be done for them by my Father in heaven. For where two or three are gathered in my name, there am I among them." If you are unable to identify people you know at this time to create your safety network, reach out to your local church and ask for someone who can pray with you. Also, join a local Bible Study group, there you should easily be able to identify people who will constantly pray for and with you.

It is important to be strengthened and encouraged by fellow believers. "As iron sharpens iron, so one person sharpens another." (Proverbs 27:17, NIV). When two pieces of iron rub against each other, neither become nor remain dull. Similarly, important relationships such as friendships and accountability partners help us stay sharp.

One way I stay sharp is by participating in Community Bible Study (CBS, 2022) and having a caring community of people who help me grow spiritually. Some members from my Bible Study class have become like family to me. Given that my family is in Florida while I reside in California, members from this community have invited me to spend holidays and other special occasions with them throughout my time in northern California.

In addition to participating in CBS, I also have a small group of young adult women I communicate and fellowship with often, known as OmniSole [which means all (Omni) single/unmarried (sole)]. We are a beautiful Christian community who share the gospel with each other, hang out and have fun, and most importantly, we hold each other accountable regarding spiritual growth and pursuing our visions. We communicate via text or group chat almost daily as well as do virtual and in-person hangouts frequently. We often check in with each other to discuss our spiritual challenges, growth areas, goals, and the accountability we need as we are pursuing our visions. This group of women is very important for encouraging me in my faith walk and my progress toward goals, including writing this book. We also help each other when needs arise, whether it is a need for advice or a ride to/from events when it is best to carpool as well as more serious needs. All of us know that we are always available for each other and that we are a strong support system for everyone in our group. Within this loving community, we engage in authentic conversations and offer each other constructive feedback to promote holistic growth in all aspects of our lives. This helps us grow in the knowledge and grace of God and spur one another on to good works that God designed for each of us.

Never be afraid to enlist the help of others, especially those you can trust. In its devotional, *Safety in Numbers*, Joel Osteen Ministries recommends ensuring "the people who are giving you advice have earned your respect as a source of wisdom. Then you need to follow your own heart in light of God's Word and do what you feel is right and good for you." It is important to have a network of wise counsel. Thankfully, participating in CBS and OmniSole gives me opportunities to offer and receive help when needed.

God has already pre-arranged for you to cross paths with certain people to help you fulfill your purpose. Those people may be influential in helping you spiritually or supporting you vocationally. Either way, having a safety network is critical for pursuing purpose. It is important to have different communities of accountability. With CBS, I have an intergenerational community of spiritually mature believers, and with OMNISOLE, I have a community of young adult women I can relate to in ways that are different from my relationships in CBS. Although these communities are very different, they both include accountability partners I can confide in as we "spur one another on toward love and good deeds." (Hebrews 10:24, NIV).

Share Your Vision

I was always familiar with Habakkuk 2:2 (ESV): "*Write the vision; make it plain on tablets, so he may run who reads it.*", but I often focused on the first part until one day I reread the verse and realized it states"*....so he may run who reads it.*"

There's a saying: "If you want to go fast, go alone. If you want to go far, go with others." Over time, I have learned that one can go far and fast alone, but the experience is enriched when others are galvanized to join. As King Solomon taught,

> Two are better than one because they have a good return for their labor; for if either of them falls, the one will lift up his companion. But woe to the one who falls when there is not another to lift him up! Furthermore, if two lie down together they keep warm, but how can one be warm *alone*? And if one can overpower him who is alone, two can resist him. A cord of three *strands* is not quickly torn apart.
>
> Ecclesiastes 4:9-12 (NASB)

Teamwork makes the dreamwork. It's important to build a team to help you fulfill your vision. Whether those you collaborate with are directly involved with your endeavors, or not, it is important to have a support system. I read a story about Scottish-American industrialist and philanthropist Andrew Carnegie who collaborated with others during his business ventures. Carnegie surrounded himself with experts who could do what he was incapable of. These were individuals with innovative ideas and others who implemented those ideas. As a result of collaborating with others, Carnegie led the expansion of the American steel industry in the late 19th century.

Sharing your vision involves networking with others to help you accomplish your goals. When you share your vision, this creates a spirit of cooperation. This also challenges and inspires others to pursue their dreams as they support what God has placed in your heart.

While writing this book, a few of my relatives and a dear friend often checked in with me to see how it was developing and to encourage me in the process. One of my relatives also connected me with another author who was willing to support me in this journey by reading and commenting on drafts to highlight details I overlooked, and as well as providing advice and encouragement regarding authorship. Additionally, my friend was my accountability partner who frequently called me to check in regarding my goals and progress. All of this support was much needed and highly appreciated!

Whether you need an accountability partner, or someone to be hands-on regarding a project, it is essential to have others around you to spur you on to good works that the Father preordained for you (Ephesians 2:10). It is important to reciprocate this as well. I often called and checked in with persons in my support system to see how they were doing and to offer encouragement regarding their endeavors. We discovered that from sharing our milestones, we inspired each other. This not only related to our vision goals, but also our self-care and overall productivity regarding other endeavors as well.

Confide with Caution

Be careful of who you confide in. Personal revelation is not meant for public reveal. In Genesis, we learn that Joseph's life involved much suffering, which initially stemmed from revealing his dream to his family (see Genesis 37-44). His siblings despised him because he was highly favored by their father, and his dream created division between him and his family. The young man was betrayed and sold into slavery by his brothers, unjustly accused by Potiphar's wife, imprisoned, and forgotten.

Only share your vision with those who believe in you and are trustworthy. Be intentional with who you share your vision with. Know who and what are essential to executing your vision.

Before sharing, ask yourself: "Who is essential to helping me fulfill my vision? What is the purpose of sharing my vision with this person? What role should this person play?" If you cannot answer all of these questions clearly, then, do not share your vision with said individual(s).

When sharing your vision with partners, be sure to clearly identify roles and expectations. Clearly articulating your vision and purposes for partnership creates identity, clarity, and meaning for all parties involved. This is critical for effective implementation. When partners know their roles, they understand how they contribute to the overall purpose for which the vision is established. This also creates and fosters a culture of clarity, cooperation, and collaboration among relationships as partners have a shared understanding of the goals and purposes for which they serve.

Communicating a clear vision to others compels them to buy in and help execute the plan. I found that those who offered moral support did not need defined roles as those developed organically from my relationships and pursuit of purpose. However, those within my network for technical support (e.g. editing, publishing, marketing, etc.) did need defined roles based on their expertise and potential contributions. You can identify who to network with based on their expertise and experiences. For example, I have friends and colleagues who are published authors. So, reaching out to them for advice throughout my writing process and beyond was very helpful. I also have colleagues who edit. So, they were also helpful. You will find that those you collaborate with will depend upon what you need to accomplish your goals.

Vision is powerful. When a vision statement or blueprint exists, one has an idea of implementation. The vision is a blueprint for people to enact. When leaders share a vision, members can buy in. The Bible says, "faith comes by hearing." (Romans 10:17, NKJV). So, when you design a blueprint for your vision you also have something tangible you can use (because you made it plain) to motivate others to help you enact it. The blueprint is not the final product. It is open to modification, but you must have something to work with. If you do not have a blueprint, pray and ask God about what He wants you to do. Also, consult with praying friends about your passions and encourage them to pray with and for you to receive clarity regarding what God is calling you to do. Keep in mind that your blueprint does not have to be elaborate or fully developed. Start with where you are. Identify goals you want to accomplish and consider journaling. Also, read about things that interest you, which will likely lead to inspiration for your pursuits. As you do these things, be sure to record what God puts in your heart and brings to mind, and you will see your blueprint begin to unfold in a clear manner for you to implement.

After identifying who you should share your vision with, execute it!

CHAPTER 12

Pursuing Your Purpose (Part 1): Activate Your Vision

God gives us the ability. He gives us creative ideas and inventions, but we have to be diligent, do our part, and step out and use what He's given us. We have to sow seed in order to see the harvest that He has promised.

Joel Osteen

What is the point of dreaming big or imagining a future you want or goals you want to reach, but never acting upon your desires? What dreams has God given you? It is so important to activate them.

In order to achieve your desired outcomes, you must be willing to work. As stated by Brian Rathbone, "Anything worth having is worth working for." In the Bible, we read that "The desire of the sluggard kills him, for his hands refuse to labor." (Proverbs 21:25, ESV). This means that when someone desires something, but refuses to work for it, that person could experience mental or emotional suffering as a result of always aspiring, but never attaining. This is because "hope deferred makes the heart sick; but when dreams come true at last, there is life and joy." (Proverbs 13:12, Living Bible). King Solomon, author of Proverbs, also wrote, "Lazy people want much but get little, but those who work hard will prosper." (Proverbs 13:4, NLT). Unlike those who desire, but never work to accomplish their desired outcomes, people who passionately pursue their dreams are likely to obtain the desires of their hearts.

Sadly, most people do not invest quality time in pursuing their goals, no matter how talented they are. Journalist Malcolm Gladwell once said, "*Talent is the ab*ility to practice.", and Coach Tim Notke challenges, "Hard work beats talent when talent fails to work hard." Talent without hard work is insufficient. One must consistently rely upon the Lord, knowing that His grace is sufficient (2 Corinthians 12:9), while working hard for goal attainment. This requires preparation.

What Are You Doing with What You Have?

Preparation is essential for pursuing purpose. Preparation is the action or process of making something ready for use, or of getting ready for some occasion (Oxford University Press, 2022c). One way to prepare is to embrace every God-given opportunity without hesitation. American track and field athlete and four-time Olympic gold medalist Jesse Owens rightly said, "One chance is all you need." You must expend determined effort toward every opportunity God gives you and be determined to bloom where you are planted.

At one point while speaking to His disciples, Jesus explained a parable about a wealthy man who entrusted three of his employees with money called talents while he went out of town (see Matthew 25:14-30). In this story, two of the employees diligently invested and managed their talents and gained double the amounts they invested, while the third employee buried his talent. Some time later, the employer returned to see what the employees did with their talents. Being pleased with the two employees who managed their talents well and produced more, the employer administered more talents to manage, but being displeased with the employee who ignored his talent by burying it in the ground, he fired him.

Like the first two employees, be diligent with what you have in your hands today. The servant who buried his talent in the earth was ignorant of what he had. Like the wealthy employer in Jesus' parable, God will provide, but you, like the employees, must steward His provision. If you are content and faithful with what you have, while also striving for more, you will reap a harvest of return, and God will entrust you with more.

The Bible says, "Every good gift and every perfect gift is from above, and comes down from the Father..." (James 1:17, NKJV). God gave you talents, or gifts and abilities, to use to fulfill your purpose and glorify Him, but what you do with your talents is up to you. Be disciplined and diligent. Go the extra mile even when you think it goes unnoticed because God honors diligence. From the servant who buried his talent, you can see that if you are undisciplined with your talents, you will waste precious time and energy. So, work hard each day as you strive toward your vision. Like the employer in the parable of the talents, God wants to reward your faithfulness, and He wants you to enjoy your work and the fruits of your labor (Ecclesiastes 5:18) as well as be proud of your effort each day. *He is good and faithful and* promises to richly supply the soul of the diligent (Proverbs 13:4).

Are you willing to put in the work to fulfill your dream? Solely believing, goal setting, and planning are not enough. You must work toward accomplishing your goals because "faith apart from works is dead." (James 2:26). As American football coach Vince Lombardi said, "The only place success comes before work is in the dictionary."

True gifts and talents are worth cultivating to the point of maturity. God's goal for your gifts is not only for them to be used, but for you to advance them. So, choose to identify, embrace, and fully develop your God-given abilities rather than neglect, waste, or fiddle with them. 1 Corinthians 10:31 (ISV) says "do everything for the glory of God." That means being and doing your best with all that God has given you—both your tangible and intangible attributes. This includes using your gifts with excellence. Author Ralph Marston once said, "Excellence is not a skill, it's an attitude."

As in the parable, the same is (true) in life. God entrusts us with gifts and talents as evident in our natural abilities. Everything He entrusts us with—His Word, time, talents, spiritual gifts, opportunities, employment, and networks—must be intentionally geared toward accomplishing the purposes He's given us. When you are faithful with what God has given you while being open to new opportunities, you position yourself for increase. Be faithful with current opportunities and do not despise small beginnings (Zechariah 4:10). When you are faithful with what you have, God will allow you to steward more (Matthew 25:23).

When I set out to write this book—my distal goal, I created countless proximal goals to achieve along the way which accompanied action. Some of the endeavors that were instrumental in me writing this book included: journaling, daily devotion, prayer (see Chapter 2), declarations (see Chapter 8), reading, and of course, writing. All of these actions contributed to my knowledge base, excitement, and motivation for writing this book, even when I did not feel like it and was unsure of how it would turn out.

Although you may not have initially planned everything out, that is okay. As you walk by faith, God will provide more clarity throughout your journey of pursuing purpose. Before I decided to write the book, I did not know that my years of daily journaling would result in this book. I also did not realize that my research skills acquired during my graduate school training would be instrumental in my identifying and analyzing content for this book. I would like to assume that like me, you have previous experiences that can inform your current goals. Perhaps you read something, conversed with someone, networked with others, participated in an event and/or attended a program or webinar to acquire knowledge and skills that are useful for attaining your goals.

After clarifying your goals and identifying experiences and resources you have acquired to contribute to your desired outcome (that aligns with what God desires for your life), you must be zealous and consistent. "Whatever you do, work heartily." (Colossians 3:23, ESV). Will you be fervent in spirit (Romans 12:11)? This is the hard part! Although I identified overarching distal goals for this book (e.g. writing, editing, and publishing) prior to beginning this project, most of my proximal goals (analyzing, organizing, etc.) developed as I was writing. In other words, the more actions I took, the more goals I developed and accomplished along the way. Action motivates you to stay focused and consistent, and it produces excitement for something to look forward to. Also, the more you work, the more you accomplish and are able to reflect upon and celebrate along the way to achieving your distal goals. So, move your feet and get to work. Start pursuing your goals!

Be Consistent

Many people approach pursuing purpose or exercising gifts in a "fits and starts" manner. However, to maintain focus and thrive, one must be consistent. This often requires establishing routines or structures conducive to prioritizing. Consistency over the long term is essential for success. Think of someone who is training for a marathon. That person must be consistent with preparation and training in order to perform well in the race. To develop endurance, one cannot afford to only workout when (s)he feels like it. Instead, (s)he must be consistent. This is necessary for training the body's muscles and overall stamina. The same way an athlete must develop a structure for consistency in order to successfully participate in a race, you have to be consistent in order to thrive in any area of your life.

Consistency will help you maintain focus on your goals and prevent deviating from them. It is not what you work on once or twice that leads to success, but what you work on consistently that leads to the desired result. Small incremental accomplishments lead to substantial success. In his book *Deep Work*, Cal Newport recommends blocking two to three hours daily without Wi-Fi and a phone to focus on work. He suggests deep work results in best work. Newport advises that maintaining a daily routine of a few hours is more effective than spending more than twice this amount of work daily focusing on shallow work.

Consistency is essential to progress. It is best to devote a fraction of time each day to focus on substantive work in achieving your goals. Daily productivity in small amounts will always lead to progress. This will accumulate into significant change over time which will culminate in attaining the desires you are pursuing. So, don't be dismayed if your progress seems slow.

CHAPTER 13

Pursuing Your Purpose (Part 2): Get Focused, Stay Focused

Where your attention goes, your time goes.

Idowu Koyenikan

Focus is a key to success. Focus, or lack thereof, is often the determining factor between success and failure. When your thoughts about fulfilling your vision and actions align over a consistent period of time, you will accomplish your goals. So, to fulfill your vision, you must stay focused because focus enacts consistent engagement.

I encounter many people who tell me they are focused, and yet, they also tell me they are divided between what seems logical, fits into their budgets, and aligns with their schedules. This tells me they may want to focus, or they try to focus, and believe they are focused, but they are not. They say they are focused, yet they are scattered between their concerns and are unable to concentrate on their desired outcomes. Realizing this has helped me understand what true focus really is. It is more than attraction. It is releasing the burden of being mentally divided between ideas or concerns. Focus is a decisive action that brings direct attention to one's soul (mind, will, and emotions).

Focus, as Pastor EB Herman (2020) says, "maintains your cognitive abilities and natural energies—keeping them together—so that you can pursue and arrive at the destination that God has set for you." Or maybe that you set for yourself under divine guidance." In other words, focus is the ability to sustain your attention and align your actions accordingly so you can accomplish your goal. To focus is to concentrate on something for an extended period of time. Pastor Herman further explains that focus is "how you think." This refers to what you give your intellectual attention to as well as the activity you engage in. Both should be congruent.

To fulfill your dreams, you have to almost daily hone your attention to accomplish your goals. This requires long periods of uninterrupted time. You have to be dogged at blocking out distractions. According to a study by Microsoft, the average attention span of a person is eight seconds; a sharp decrease of 12 seconds from the year 2000 (Cision, 2018). Focus requires quieting your mind and filtering out anything that pulls your attention away from pursuing your purpose. This may be challenging for people who work long hours, have young children, or engage in other time-consuming demands. However, it is important to block out space and time throughout the week to focus on a passion project. This could be early in the morning before everyone else awakes, or in the evening after everyone is asleep.

You must be intentional to put the activity of focus on your calendar or in your planner as well as set an alarm to ensure that you follow through with it. If it helps, identify an accountability partner who can check in with you throughout the week and help you assess your weekly goals. Keep in mind that you might not be able to spend hours at a time, and that it is okay. The key is to be intentional about working toward your goals with the amount of time that you are able to allot to that. What you choose to do during your personal time is your choice. It may vary from one session to the next. Create an outline or to-do list to identify what you want to accomplish. Be sure to establish SMART goals, or objectives that are: specific, measurable, achievable, relevant, and time bound (Atlassian, 2022). When you create practical goals, you are likely to accomplish them.

What interferes with focus? Distraction and procrastination. We live in a world with countless distractions.

Negative thinking in the forms of doubt, fear of failure, or the opinions of others are common distractions that result in being stagnant or going in the wrong direction. According to the Oxford dictionary (2022d), doubt is a feeling of uncertainty or fear.

Why do we doubt? Perhaps it is because we are unsure or afraid of a future outcome. Maybe it is because we experience opposition. This could be in the forms of others' opinions, not seeing how our dreams will unfold, or not having all of the resources upfront to fulfill our dreams. Perhaps opposition tempts us to doubt God's sovereignty or omnipotence. When we are uncertain, we are often tempted to doubt what we know to be true. In the Old Testament, speaking to Israel at Mount Carmel, Elijah said, "How long will you waver between two opinions? If the Lord is God, follow Him; but if Baal, follow him. But the people said nothing" (See 1 Kings 18:21, NIV).

Doubt and fear are friends, and both result in negative thinking, interfering with focus. Doubt and fear are paralyzing. As you can see in 1 Kings 18:21, after Elijah posed the question, the people remained silent. Although they knew who the God of Israel was, they were lukewarm. They wanted to experience rain after a three-year drought as a result of Elijah's prayers, but they also wanted to serve Baal—an idol god. God's word teaches us that "a double-minded man is unstable in all his ways." (James 1:8, KJV). This is what doubt and fear do. They lead to instability and paralyzation. They cause us to lose focus on our dreams by dwelling on circumstances and lavishing our attention elsewhere instead of on God, particularly His will and promises. Doubt and fear are distractions.

It is not God's will for you to be pressed down with doubt because of uncertainty. He desires that your mind be at rest. God delights in giving you peace and will do so when you focus on Him and what He is doing. He wants to partner with you and help you stay focused. Isaiah 26:3 (NIV) says it this way:

> "You will keep in perfect peace those whose minds are steadfast, because they trust in you."

A steadfast mind produces stability. To maintain focus, you must trust God and learn to doubt your doubts. Scripture teaches us to forsake negative thinking by bringing every wrong thought captive and submitting it to Christ's authority (2 Corinthians 10:5). When doubt creeps in, change the channel in your mind and choose to focus only on what is excellent and praiseworthy (Philippians 4:8). God gives us the ability to think positively, but we must be intentional to maintain positive thoughts by refusing to allow doubt to interfere with our focus.

Let's look at Jesus as the ultimate example of staying focused. For the joy set before Him, He endured the cross and despised the shame (Hebrews 12:2). In other words, Jesus did not allow trouble to distract Him from His ultimate goal—saving mankind. Instead, He focused on the outcome. He focused on our redemption. He did not allow trouble to distract Him from God's intent. He kept His eyes on His purpose and God's promise. He kept His eyes on the prize!

Doubts are inevitable, but they must not dominate your decisions. I once read that doubt kills more dreams than failure ever will. Don't allow wrong thinking to limit your dreams. If you think you'll never accomplish your goals or don't have the ability, the network or the funds, then you are limiting your dreams by dwelling on the wrong things. No matter what is happening in the economy, keep your eyes fixed on God, knowing that His plan is always for your good. Set your mind on what He says in His word, not the stock market. If you fix your eyes and mind on the promises of God, you will eventually experience the manifestations of those promises. See yourself as God sees you. You know how He sees you as a result of staying in His word. When you regard the word, your focus becomes clearer. Let His word drive your decision-making.

God expects you to trust Him. What does He say about you and your present situation? Think about those things! There's a song by Hillsong entitled, "I Am Who You Say I Am." Focus on what God says about you. What has He promised you? Remember, God's promises never return void (Isaiah 55:11). You just have to align with the word and stay focused on pursuing what He has for you.

Continually refine Your focus. Stay focused by remaining fixated on your vision. "Let your eyes look straight ahead; fix your gaze directly before you. Give careful thought to the paths for your feet and be steadfast in all your ways. Do not turn to the right or the left..." (Proverbs 4:25-27, NIV). Do not focus on what you cannot see or do not have. Instead, focus on what you want to see and what you do have. These could be tangibles or intangibles. Focus on creating and pursuing clear goals. Focus on the people you are serving or will serve as you accomplish your goals. Focus on doing your current job with excellence and focus on maximizing your resources.

Everything you need to focus on already exists in tangible or intangible forms. Stay focused on pursuing your purpose with excellence. Stay focused on putting your family first. Stay focused on investing resources in your dream. Stay focused on finishing school. Stay focused on entrepreneurship. Don't take a half-hearted approach. Put forth your best effort in fulfilling your dream.

One of the ways you can discern that you are truly focused, rather than merely trying to focus, is how you respond to criticism. If you say you are focused but continue to worry about other people's opinions regarding our dreams, then, you are not fixated on your vision. You may be attempting to, but you are not yet focused. When you are fixated on something, you cannot be moved because your determination fuels your focus.

Do not let others set limits for your calling. You do not need anyone to validate you to do what God calls you to do. You are never limited by the opinions of others nor confined to the criticisms of your critics. So, don't see yourself the way other people see you. Do not let others' opinions cause you to lose focus. Don't allow others to hinder you nor frustrate your purpose. Do not let others limit your dreams!

On many occasions, Jesus did not respond when others criticized and ridiculed Him as He was following the Father's will. He often ignored naysayers. Like Jesus, you must not lose focus of the goals set before you. Not everyone will agree with or support you, but that is okay. If God is for you, who can be against you? (Romans 8:31). What can prevail against you? No weapon! (Isaiah 54:17). Remember, you do not have to argue with nor try to convince people of your dreams because you and God are a majority!

There will always be naysayers, but do not let what they say, tweet, or post stop you from moving forward to fulfill your dreams. Soon, you will realize that more people are for you than against you. There are people who need you to fulfill your dreams so they can be inspired to pursue theirs. Also, think about the people you will help as a result of fulfilling your dreams. Focus on that continually. Let that far outweigh what any negative critic says.

As you are focused on pursuing your dreams, opposition will come, but fear not. Opposition is anything that attempts to hinder fulfillment of your purpose. Look at opposition as an opportunity to strengthen your focus, not a reason to relinquish it or give up. While opposition may appear, it does not have to prevail. The enemy will often tempt you to doubt God or what He is doing on your behalf. It is important to recognize distractions, but refuse to allow them to interfere with God's will for your life. Seize control of your thoughts. Center your attention. Don't allow negative thoughts to linger. Take them captive! In Ephesians (6:13-17) and Philippians (4:8-9), Paul tells how to do this as he urges readers to stand firm against the enemy. The apostle encourages thinking the right thoughts.

I once heard someone say, "You are what you eat." This applies spiritually just as much, if not more, than it does physically. It is imperative to constantly meditate on those things which are pure, lovely, virtuous, and of good report (Philippians 4:8). As you meditate on those things, your mind will crave more and more of the substance. Therefore, you must keep your mind stayed on Christ and monitor your thoughts by filtering out the ungodly ones. You alone are responsible for the thoughts you choose to cultivate. Choose to establish healthy thought patterns as you combat negative thoughts by concentrating on what the Word says about you. The more you learn to stay focused despite opposition, the easier it will be to ignore distractions and move past them as you pursue purpose.

Procrastination

While distractions are inevitable, procrastination is under your control. There's a saying, "do not put off for tomorrow what you can do today." One thing that contributes to procrastination is how a person feels. Often, a person must be in the mood to engage in an activity. Other times, a person may decide to mis prioritize while procrastinating.

While preparing for my qualifying exams, I often read articles and watched scholarly videos to inform my research. However, when it was time to write, everything became a blur. Why? Because I enjoyed reading, but put off writing (the main thing I would be evaluated upon). So, I engaged in productive procrastination. This occurs when a person delays engaging in an activity that should be prioritized to focus on something else. The activity one chooses to focus on may be necessary to complete eventually, but it is not urgent or more pressing than the primary task which should be the primary focus.

It was not until I stopped procrastinating and prioritized effectively that I created and stuck to a plan to successfully pass my comprehensive exams.

Time is of the essence. A truly focused person does not procrastinate, but redeems the time. One way to use time efficiently is to create a to-do list each night for the following day. Outline timeframes in your calendar for each task, and check off each activity as you complete it. Provide breaks throughout your activities. Perhaps you can implement the Pomodoro Technique daily (Boorgard, 2022) by setting a timer to work within 25-minute intervals followed by five-minute breaks after each working interval. After each fourth interval, break for 15-20 minutes. This will help you maximize time throughout each day as you work toward accomplishing your goals.

CHAPTER 14

You Have a Purpose!

Only God's will has the ability to satisfy us. We are created for Him and for His purposes, and anything less than that is totally incapable of bringing lasting contentment.

Joyce Meyer

Before the foundation of the world, God had a plan for your life. He created you with and for purpose, and He created you to be successful! God specifically gifted you with everything you need to pursue and fulfill the purpose He created you for. You have everything you need to accomplish your goals and fulfill your vision. You have the inspiration, insight, and innovation to be successful.

Not only did God equip you for success, He also orchestrated opportunities and key people that are pivotal to your pursuit of purpose.

One key to discovering and fulfilling your purpose is identifying your passion. Passion enacts pursuit. It is your passion for what God called you to do that drives your pursuit of purpose. When you are passionate, you begin with a definite purpose and set defined goals and plans for achieving them. That's because passion is intentional and unstoppable! Passion is what motivates you despite the obstacles you encounter. It survives any disappointment or discouragement you encounter and perceives any defeat as only temporary. It even survives burnout. Passion also outweighs criticism and motivates you to succeed in spite of it.

Keys to stirring your God-given passion are praying and spending time in the word. Whether you're at home, work, on lunch break, in the uber, or waiting for an appointment, take time to pray and read scripture daily, throughout the day. Meditate on the word and verbally declare it daily. The word of God keeps your priorities aligned with God's will for your life. As you read and meditate on scripture, the Holy Spirit replaces your desires with God's desires for you. Instead of living according to your own agenda, you will aim to glorify God by aligning your priorities with His will. Spending time in prayer and the word will reveal who you are, what you have, and what you can do. Throughout this process, God will give you wisdom, guidance, and patience to align with His will—the safest, best, wisest, and happiest place to be.

The only way to be sure you are walking correctly is to follow the One who knows the way perfectly. The Lord is willing and able to guide you if you allow Him. Choose to follow Him by reading and applying the word to your life. Also, pray regarding both big and small decisions to remain on the path He has for you. You must seek His timing and direction in all things instead of what seems logical (Proverbs 3:5-6). Never act outside of His timing nor without His direction. Refuse to act upon impulse. As Scottish Baptist evangelist and teacher Oswald Chambers warns, "if you have the slightest doubt, then He is not guiding. Whenever there is doubt-wait." Your heart may make plans, but allow God to direct you, for He will establish you as you commit your way to Him (see Proverbs 16:1-9).

God has a plan mapped out for you (Jeremiah 29:11), and He is leading you to fulfill your purpose. One psalmist summed up, "your word is a lamp unto my feet, and a light unto my path." (Psalms 119:109, KJV). Often, we think of a well-lit path when we read this passage. However, a lamp highlights each area before you take each step rather than illuminating the full path at once. It is a step-by-step guide on an unknown path. In Touch Ministries (2019a) sums this up so well in its devotional, *How To Discern Direction From God*, "Since God's Word is a light to our path, the more we think about the truths of Scripture, the clearer the way will become."(Psalm 119:105). God wants to guide you each step of the way as you pursue purpose, for He knows your final destination and the best way for you to arrive there. So, stay focused, and He will enlighten your every step to bring you across the right people and resources at the appropriate time.

Fully Committed

You cannot expect to thrive by happenstance. Both success and failure are largely due to habit. However, success requires commitment and discipline.

Pursuing purpose requires commitment. This means you are wholeheartedly engaged in fulfilling God's plan for your life despite the obstacles you encounter. The thought of committing to something long-term, especially when it's challenging, can be dreadful. When we experience things that are frustrating or demanding, we want instant relief. However, when you are committed, you are tenacious in your pursuit. You are all in!

Jesus is the perfect example of commitment. He knew His purpose and didn't allow difficulty to deter Him. He stayed focused and determined to accomplish His goal—to give His life so that we may have eternal life. He never abandoned His call as ordained by the heavenly Father. Instead, He finished the work God committed to Him, no matter the cost. Simply put, Jesus persevered.

The word "persevere" is interesting. It is a military term that can be translated as *"don't abandon your post"* (Stanley, 2014). It could be used to describe the guard of Jews established day and night in Jerusalem when their enemies conspired against them after they began rebuilding the wall in the city (see Nehemiah 4:7-18). The image of commitment and perseverance show up in 2 Chronicles as well, during the time Asa expelled idolatry throughout Judah, Benjamin, and Ephraim (see 2 Chronicles 15:2-18). Through Obed, the spirit of God promised Asa, Benjamin, and Judah that perseverance would be rewarded (2 Chronicles 2:7), and the Apostle Paul told the same thing to Timothy—his son in the faith (1 Timothy 6:12) and the Romans (Romans 5:3-5). Perhaps this inspired the words of the Apostle James, "let perseverance finish its work so that you may be mature and complete, not lacking anything.", he urged Jewish Christians dispersed outside of Israel (James 1:4, NIV). The same image was depicted again when the apostle Peter told God's elect to persevere (2 Peter 1:6), which would contribute to the effectiveness and productivity in confirming their calling.

In every instance, perseverance is essential to fulfilling purpose as ordained by God. In a devotional entitled, *Perseverance in Suffering*, I once read, "When we choose not to give up during difficult circumstances, we allow God to build up good qualities in our life that will keep us going in the long term." (ITM, 2019d). This demonstrates character and hope. Perseverance and commitment are all about refusing to quit in order to complete an assignment.

To fulfill your God-given purpose, you have to determine that you are going to commit to what God called you to do. As the Creator, He is the only One truly worthy of your complete devotion and the One whose approval really matters. You have to diligently and completely give yourself to obeying the Father and forsake anything that could hinder your pursuit of purpose. When your goals align with His plan for your life, He will help you achieve them and acquire true success.

True Success

Success refers to the accomplishment of an aim or purpose. This requires discipline, for it is discipline, not desire (only) that determines your destiny. Discipline is the link between desire and accomplishment. Scripture frequently compares life to a race and emphasizes the importance of discipline for fulfilling purpose.

The only success that matters is accomplishing the purpose God created you for. As clearly stated in the devotional *Remembering God's Priority,* "to be successful in God's eyes, it's critical that we keep His priorities as our own and make continual course corrections to stay on track." Pursuing purpose is a process. Arthur Ashe brilliantly said, "Success is a journey, not a destination...." It is the process of pursuing purpose by which life lessons are learned. God uses the process of pursuing purpose and the circumstances you encounter to cultivate your spiritual growth, character development, and practical skills essential for success. The goal of pursuing purpose is God's glory, not self-glory. So, success is determined by how you use what God has entrusted you with to honor Him. Every good gift from God is meant to draw you closer to Him and fulfill His plan for your life. As you pursue purpose, it is important to not lose sight of the One who gave you the purpose as you focus on fulfilling it. So, remember Whose you are.

Choose to effectively steward your resources and aim to glorify the Lord with a spirit of excellence and diligence, for "the desires of the diligent are fully satisfied." (Proverbs 13:4, NIV).

Created For Purpose

What breaks your heart? What sets your heart ablaze? What can you offer to improve your community? Questions like these lead us to where "[our] deep gladness and the world's deep hunger meet," as Theologian Frederick Buechner wrote, and push us toward pursuing purpose.

What does it mean to pursue purpose? Another name for purpose is call. Answering the call, or pursuing purpose comes down to knowing why you exist. Oswald Chambers (1992) writes, "The call is the expression of the nature of the One who calls....The call of God is the expression of God's nature." On the sixth day, God said, "Let us make man in our image, after our likeness." (Genesis 1:26, ESV). Moreover, "For those whom He foreknew He also predestined to be conformed to the image of His Son....And those whom He predestined He also called....." (Romans 8:29-30, ESV). God's call for each person is to allow His Son to be revealed from within.

God designed humanity to be like The Trinity-one Being in three unique, not unconnected persons. Each person is a three-part being—-spirit, soul, and body, reflecting the triune God—Father, Son, and Spirit. God's purpose is for the world to see an invisible Deity through visible images. He is looking for people to represent Him on earth with words, attitudes, and actions that glorify Him and edify others. Our job as His ambassadors is to reflect His image to the world by imitating Christ and revealing His heart.

In the year that King Uzziah died, Isaiah saw the Lord and overheard Him ask, "Whom shall I send? And who will go for us?", and he willingly responded to God's call (see Isaiah 6:1-8). Some time later, Isaiah openly confessed,

> "The Spirit of the Lord God is upon me, because the Lord has anointed and commissioned me to bring good news to the humble and afflicted; He has sent me to bind up [the wounds of] the brokenhearted, to proclaim release [from confinement and condemnation] to the [physical and spiritual] captives and freedom to prisoners...."
>
> (Isaiah 61:1, AMP)

Jesus recognized this confession, which was written in a script given to Him to read in the synagogue in Nazareth (see Luke 4:16-21). Fortunately, many would turn to Christ-all because Isaiah boldly volunteered to be sent by God.

What is God calling you to do? Are you reluctantly holding back, or faithfully moving forward? Will you choose to be like Isaiah and Jesus and faithfully respond to God's call-to be sent to open people's eyes so that they may turn from darkness to light?

Pursuing purpose requires determination to live absolutely and entirely for the Lord. It means doing exactly what He wants you to do as a result of surrendering your life to Christ absolutely and irrevocably. It requires a continual willingness to submit your will to His. "Service to God is the deliberate love-gift of a nature that has heard the call of God," Oswald Chambers (1992) affirms.

Your God-given purpose is the reason for which you were created and exist. It is the essence of the Father's intention or objective for you to fulfill. God equipped you with everything you need to fulfill His will, and He works in you to do what pleases Him (see Hebrews 13:21). He uniquely created you (your personality) and equipped you (with strengths, abilities, talents, and experiences) to live according to His plan for your life. It is He who works in you to live according to His good pleasure (Philippians 2:13). He directs your mind and orchestrates your logic and plans to glorify Him.

Before the foundation of the earth, God knew you, planned for you and chose you! When God created you, He also created the "good works" for you to do throughout your life (Ephesians 2:10 [NIV]). He carefully created your natural features and gave you gifts and talents to glorify Him. God lovingly and carefully created you in His image for this time and place (see Psalms 139; Acts 17:26). You are His masterpiece. He created you on purpose and for a purpose. Until heaven, you are to do the works He prepared beforehand (see Ephesians 1:4; 2:10). Doing so results in living with purpose, on purpose, and for purpose!

Pursuing Purpose

Life is meant to be a pursuit of purpose. A life well lived is one in which purpose is fulfilled. When we choose this existence, we guarantee ourselves the finest that God has to offer and discover that it is the greatest reward of all. The greatest joy of our heavenly Father's heart is knowing that we, His sons and daughters, are pursuing purpose. He is proud to call us purpose pursuers.

A definite purpose must be identified before being fulfilled. The goal of pursuing purpose is to serve God with your whole being according to His will for your life as He guides you. God has already laid out the plan for your life. He knows exactly what you need and when you need it. Seeking Him and His instruction from His Word is what edifies and equips you to fulfill the purpose He predestined you for.

I have enjoyed writing this book, and I pray you enjoyed reading it. I hope this text inspires you to pursue purpose in all things and at all times. Dream it, believe it, live it! I believe your final chapter concludes with you fulfilling your God-given purpose.

ARE YOU PURSUING YOUR PURPOSE?

Just beyond our last heartbeat lies eternity.

Charles Stanley

Your entire life is designed to be a pursuit of your God-given purpose, which begins with a personal relationship with Jesus Christ. This happens when you give Him Lordship of your life by recognizing Him as your Savior and by continually obeying Him. He has a unique purpose for you with your unique personality, abilities, and qualities in mind. Pursuing purpose requires submitting to God's guidance for your life according to His sovereign will. It is only then that you will be complete, content, and fulfilled.

The heavenly Father has a perfect plan for your life and a purpose for you to fulfill. You were created with God-given talents to do great things! In His infinite love and wisdom, He designed you with a purpose that only you can fulfill. Sadly, it is easy to become overwhelmed with life's demands and challenges you encounter (directly or indirectly.) It is also easy to become bombarded with and distracted by the countless promises the world offers, but has no power to provide. If you are living to satisfy your own desires, you will discover that nothing you do will ever be enough and eventually become disappointed. It is only by pursuing the good works God has prepared for you that you will experience fulfillment because that is what He created you to do.

We are invited to pursue purpose, and by doing so, we live the lives God predestined for us. Will you choose to pursue (your God-given) purpose?

NOTES

1. Abraham Lincoln Quotes, Goodreads https://www.goodreads.com/quotes/24046-the-best-thing-about-the-future-is-that-it-comes
2. Anonymous. (2021). Make time to do your best work. https://thedolectures.com/blogs/blog/make-time-to-do-your-best-work
3. Atlassian (2022). How to write SMART goals. Retrieved on June 8, 2022 from https://www.atlassian.com/blog/productivity/how-to-write-smart-goals
4. Blue Letter Bible (2022). H1897 - hāḡâ - Strong's Hebrew lexicon (kjv) - Blue Letter Bible. Retrieved June 8, 2022 from https://www.blueletterbible.org/lexicon/h1897/kjv/wlc/0-1/
5. Boorgaard, K. (2022). Take it from someone who hates productivity hacks-the Pomodoro Technique actually works.Retrieved on May 23, 2022 from https://www.themuse.com/advice/take-it-from-someone-who-hates-produtiity-hacksthe-pomodoro-technique-actually-works#:~:text=Using%20this%20method%2C%20you%20break,in-stills%20a%20sense%20of%20urgency.
6. BrainyQuote. (2021-2022). Saint Augustine quote. Retrieved on July 8, 2022 from https://www.brainyquote.com/quotes/saint_augustine_121380
7. Flavel, J. (n.d.). Brainy Quote (2021-2022). Retrieved on July 6, 2022 from https://www.brainyquote.com/quotes/john_flavel_399277#:~:text=John%20Flavel%20Quotes&text=Man's%20ex-tremity%20is%20God's%20opportunity.,-John%20Flavel
8. Butler, R.B. (2017). Walk this way. https://www.joshuaryanbutler.com/2017/03/walk-this-way/
9. Cain, J. (n.d.). The gift of no. https://www.intouch.org/read/magazine/faith-works/the-gift-of-no

10. Caine, C. (2018). Fine tune your hearing Part 3. https://www.youtube.com/watch?v=nG-WOOuRt2pU
11. CBS. (2022). Community Bible Study. Home | Community Bible Study. © 2022 COMMUNITY BIBLE Chambers, C.(1992). *My utmost for his highest: An updated edition in today's language*. In Reimann J. (ed). *The Golden Book of Oswald Chambers.* Oswald Chambers Publications.
12. Cision Contributor (2018). In Comms Best Practices. Retrieved December 31, 2020 from https://www.cision.com/2018/01/declining-attention-killing-content-marketing-strategy/
13. Coelho, P. (n.d.). Quote by Paulo Coehlo. https://www.garyfox.co/quotes/remember-dreams-fight-must-know-want-life-just-one-thing-makes-dream-become-impossible-fear-failure/
14. Collins, B. (2020). The pomodoro technique explained https://www.forbes.com/sites/bryancollinseurope/2020/03/03/the-pomodoro-technique/?sh=2a25732f3985
15. Copeland, K. (n.d.). Faith words turn your victory loose. https://sermons.love/kenneth-copeland/6420-kenneth-copeland-faith-words-turn-your-victory-loose.html
16. Eagle Mountain International Church Inc. (2018). Words—The Start Button to Everything You're Believing For. KennethCopeland Ministries (1997 - 2022).
17. Elevation Worship (2014). I will look up. https://www.youtube.com/watch?v=tEQnoE7SnZw
18. Goodreads (2022). Quote by Abraham Lincoln https://www.goodreads.com/quotes/24046-the-best-thing-about-the-future-is-that-it-comes
19. Herman, E.B. (2020), Come see a man. https://www.youtube.com/watch?v=Dv_w_lmtLqo
20. Herman, E.B. (2020). Focus thinking produces winners.10am, 062820B. https://www.youtube.com/watch?v=pJv8jyjYOJs
21. Herman (n.d.). [Sermon Quotes].
22. Herodotus Quotes. (n.d.). BrainyQuote.com. Retrieved March 21, 2022, from BrainyQuote.com Web site: https://www.brainyquote.com/quotes/herodotus_101480
23. Hilliard, I.V. (2015). Tweet. Hootsuite. Retrieved on july 5, 2022 from https://twitter.com/bishophilliard/status/641286661423374336
24. In Touch Ministries. (2019). Your daily devotion: How to discern direction from God.
25. In Touch Ministries (2019).Your daily devotion: Live according to the spirit
26. In Touch Ministries. (2019). Your daily devotion: Our struggle with the flesh:
27. In Touch Ministries. (2019). Your daily devotion: Perseverance in suffering.

28. In Touch Ministries. (2019). Your daily devotion: Remembering God's priority.

29. In Touch Ministries. (2019). Your daily devotion: The source of discernment.

30. In Touch Ministries. (n.d.). He left us a book. God's great purpose. https://www.intouch.org/listen/featured/gods-great-purpose-part1?=&Source=D000000029&utm_source=D000000029&utm_medium=email&utm_source=In+Touch+Ministries&utm_campaign=cf60842630-EMAIL_CAMPAIGN_2019_04_01_01_48&utm_medium=email&utm_term=0_6f8407989c-cf60842630-42869725

31. Israel & New Breed. (2011). No limits: Enlarge my territory-take the limits off. https://www.youtube.com/watch?v=G5gMiYGG5AE

32. Jesse Owens Quotes. (n.d.). BrainyQuote.com. Retrieved March 21, 2022, from BrainyQuote.com Web site: https://www.brainyquote.com/quotes/jesse_owens_159451

33. Joel Osteen Ministries (2019). Today's word with Joel & Victoria: Safety in numbers.

34. Lee, G. (2020). The science behind "Think and Grow Rich" and why it works. Retrieved January 3, 2020 from https://www.forbes.com/sites/ellevate/2020/01/22/the-science-behind-think-and-grow-rich-and-why-it-works/?sh=48173349699b

35. LibQuotes (2022). Oswald Chambers Quote. Retrieved July 8, 2022 from https://libquotes.com/oswald-chambers/quote/lba3a1m

36. Lovelace, P. (2021). God's grace through giving. https://subsplash.com/centeredlifetv/sermons/mi/+pt62sfm

37. Margaret J. Wheatley Quotes. (n.d.). BrainyQuote.com. Retrieved March 21, 2022, fromBrainyQuote.com Web site: https://www.brainyquote.com/quotes/margaret_j_wheatley_283933

38. Marston, R. (n.d.). Brainy Quote (2021-2022). Retrieved on July 7, 2022 from https://www.brainyquote.com/quotes/ralph_marston_104215

39. Michael Jr: (2015). Know your why. https://www.youtube.com/watch?v=LZe5y2D60YU

40. Moreland, J.P. (2005). Love your God with all your mind: The role of reason in the life of the soul.

41. Oxford University Press (2022). Oxford Languages and Google. Retrieved from https://www.google.com/search?q=define+obedience&rlz=1C1GCEA_enUS764US764&oq=define+obedience&aqs=chrome..69i57j0i512l9.4357j1j15&sourceid=chrome&ie=UTF-8

42. Oxford University Press (2022). Oxford Languages and Google. Retrieved from https://www.google.com/search?q=define+Trust+&rlz=1C1GCEA_enUS764US764&sxsrf=AL-iCzsai4tzvE7aymNI15dVeNInfK7xjSA%3A1654725510622&ei=hhuhYtLIJYi2uv-QPjNulgAw&ved=0ahUKEwjSo4vy7J74AhUIm44IHYxt-CcAQ4dUDCA4&uact=5&oq=define+Trust+&gs_lcp=Cgdnd3Mtd2l6EAMyBQ-gAEIAEMgYIABAeEAcyBggAEB4QBzIGCAAQHhAHMgYIABAeEAcyBggAEB4QBzIG-CAAQHhAHMgUIABCABDIGCAAQHhAHMgUIABCABDoHCAAQRxCwAzo-ECAAQQzoFCAAQkQI6DQgAEIAEEIcCELEDEBQ6CAgAEIAEELEDOgQIABANS-gQIQRgASgQIRhgAUPvAKVialipg5ZgqaARwAXgAgAF5iAGNB5IBAzkuMZgBAK-ABAqABAcgBCMABAQ&sclient=gws-wiz

43. Oxford University Press (2022). Oxford Languages and Google. Retrieved from https://www.google.com/search?q=doubt+definition&rlz=1C1GCEA_enUS764US764&sxsrf=ALiCzsbBGmsBT0R7HEWjRi7Zd

44. Oxford University Press (2022). Oxford Languages and Google. Retrieved from https://www.google.com/search?q=define+Preparation+&rlz=1C1GCEA_enUS764US764&sxsrf=AL-iCzsbfD30Dpylf3FKFhbK-0-MN7iyh9g%3A1654730597209&ei=ZS-hYveuDIjDuvQPvqK-

45. Permberton, R. (2014). Frederick Buechner on calling: Your deep gladness & the world's deep hunger.http://www.calledthejourney.com/blog/2014/12/17/frederick-buechner-on-calling

46. Petrides, M., Francesco, T., Yeterian, E.H., Pandya, D.N. (2012). *The frontal cortex.* In: Mai JK and Paxinos G, eds. *TheHuman Nervous System.* (3rd ed). New York: Elsevier; 2012. DOI: 10.1016/j.cortex.2011.07.002

47. Reddan at al. (2018). Attenuating neural threat expression with imagination. Retrieved Mar 3,2020 fromhttps://www.cell.com/action/showPdf?pii=S0896-6273%2818%2930955-3

48. Ruin, T. (2017). By rote: Windows to the soul.https://www.intouch.org/read/magazine/margin-notes/by-rote-windows-to-the-soul

49. Sanctus Real (2018). Confidence. https://www.youtube.com/watch?v=KA9kSBv1QrI

50. Siddiqui, S. V., Chatterjee, U., Kumar, D., Siddiqui, A., & Goyal, N. (2008). Neuropsychology of prefrontal cortex. Indian journal of psychiatry, 50(3), 202–208. https://doi.org/10.4103/0019-5545.43634

51. Stanley, C. (2014). One faith, seven virtues. https://www.intouch.org/read/one-faith-seven-virtues

52. Stanley, C. (2021). Patience-essential to experiencing God's best. Patience - Essential To Experiencing God's Best

53. Stanley, C. (2021). Walking in love-Part 1 https://www.intouch.org/listen/featured/walking-in-love-part1?=&Source=D000000045&utm_source=D000000045&utm_medium=email&utm_source=In+Tou

54. Stanley, C. (2021). Christian friendship. Radio sermon. Retrieved on September 5, 2021 fromhttps://www.intouch.org/listen/radio/christian-friendship

55. Vine, W. (24 Jun, 1996). Meditate - Vine's Expository Dictionary of New Testament Words. Retrieved fromhttps://www.blueletterbible.org/search/dictionary/viewtopic.cfm

APPENDIX

1. Discipleship Ministries. (2022). Spiritual gifts inventory. https://www.umcdiscipleship.org/spiritual-gifts-inventory/en
2. Evangelical Lutheran Church in America. (2022). Spiritual gifts assessment tool. https://www.elca.org/ourwork/congregations-and-synods/faith-practices/spiritual-renewal/assessment-tools
3. GiftsTest.com (2022). Gifts test. https://giftstest.com/
4. Lifeway Staff (2015). Spiritual gifts assessment tool: Discover your God-given spiritual gifts. 2001–2022 LifewayChristian Resources. https://www.lifeway.com/en/articles/women-leadership-spiritual-gifts-growth-service
5. Spiritual gift assessment http://brewsterchurch.com/resources/spiritual-gift-assessment
6. Spiritual Gifts Test Inventory Assessment. https://mintools.com/spiritual-gifts-test.htm
7. Team Ministry Gifted to Serve. (2022). Church Growth.org https://gifts.churchgrowth.org/spiritual-gifts-survey/
8. Gallup Inc. (2022). CliftonStrengths. Retrieved on December 9, 2022 fromhttps://www.gallup.com/cliftonstrengths/en/253850/cliftonstrengths-forindividuals.aspx?utm_source=google&utm_medium=cpc&utm_campaign=california_us_strengths_brand-

edcsecomutmterm=strengthsfinder%20assess-ment&gclid=Cj0KCQiA1suc-BhDgARIsAFoytUvr66DBzfz36rSniF9qEPxk-wovPWJ_mUuy-bWgDRZdp2yEaCTMH2bwaAgUqEALw_wcB

9. Hightest. (2022). StrengthsFinder & CliftonStrengths test - free strengths test alternative. Retrieved onDecember 9, 2022 from https://high5test.com/strengthsfinder-free/
10. Personality Assessment Resource. NERIS Analytics Limited. (2021-2022). Free personality test: NERIS typeexplorer. Retrieved on December 9, 2022 from https://www.16personalities.com/free-personality-test

Dr. Lois Harmon is an author, speaker, and an educator as well as the Founder and CEO of IMPACT (Influencing & Motivating People According to Christ's Teachings). She is also a senior leader, young adult leader, and sub core leader in her local Community Bible Study (CBS) class as well as a member of the Strategic Planning Team for CBS North America, and she helps co-lead the singles' ministry at her church. Lois holds a Ph.D. in Education with an emphasis in Leadership and Organizations from UC Santa Barbara and a B.S. in Elementary Education from Florida A&M University. She currently resides in northern California and loves to hear from readers (about how they are pursuing purpose). Connect with her on Facebook and/or visit loisharmon.com for more information.

Printed in the USA
CPSIA information can be obtained
at www.ICGtesting.com
CBHW021040301124
18256CB00011B/181